BLESSINGS
of
HOPE & JOY

by
Jan Elkins

with
Anna Elkins

Listening Heart
PO Box 509
Jacksonville, OR 97530 USA
jan@livingwatersmedford.org
ISBN-13: 978-0692975602
ISBN-10: 0692975608

Cover design by Anna Elkins

Printed in the United States of America

DEDICATION

I dedicate this book to my family:
past, present, and future.

Also by Jan Elkins with Anna Elkins:

A Book of Blessings
Blessings for Love & War

CONTENTS

FOREWORD

It is a tremendous honor to write these words of introduction for my wife's third book of blessings.

For the last 37 years, Jan and I have ministered together in many different settings. In eternity we will see the tremendous contribution her life has made in the assignments we have experienced together as husband and wife.

In the last three years since Jan has been writing her books of blessings, our family has been the recipient of God's Word imparted as a blessing. These Scriptures have been prophetic—offering words of encouragement, reminders of God's heart and His ways, and always instilling hope in our hearts.

On our frequent travels ministering in a variety of churches and conferences, Jan will often join me to give a word of blessing. When she does, something beautiful and unusual takes place. I have seen the entire atmosphere of a room shift as she declares a blessing. Jan speaks as an anointed and trusted mother in the faith.

You hold in your hand a spiritually potent book. When blessings are crafted and declared from the unchanging truth of Scripture, they release a remarkable power and anointing.

An added blessing for me is to see my daughter, Anna—our wise and faithful editor—join my wife in the creation of this book. Anna has "the touch." She can take an author's words and give them flow and balance. Both of these women live daily in the fresh and rarified air of revelation. God uses them to release beautifully crafted images of His love.

I have a feeling these blessings will still be read a hundred years from now. They are timeless in their truths and presentation. What you are about to read draws from eternity's stockpile of blessings.

Receive these well-crafted and Spirit-breathed words into your spirit, soul, and body. I bless you with a personal transformation—a transformation that comes when you know you are blessed.

Garris Elkins
Jacksonville, Oregon

INTRODUCTION

I stared with fascination at the plate sitting in front of me. It was a typical meal in the southern state of Georgia: everything was fried, including the string beans. And whatever wasn't fried was a starch.

I was visiting my alma mater, Toccoa Falls High School, for the first time since 1969. I learned more than algebra and English at that high school. I learned gratitude there.

As teenagers, my brother and I had traveled from El Salvador, Central America—where we had grown up with our missionary family—to the United States. We were to attend Toccoa Falls, a boarding school. I was new to the state of Georgia and to the South in general. We had no other family or friends or even acquaintances there. I was a thirteen-year-old freshman.

I was also a foreigner in a strange land—with strange, heavy food. Like every other student, I started to put on weight. Until then, I had never heard discussions about weight problems. Healthy eating was not a topic of conversation in the 1960s.

Gradually, by the end of my freshman year, none of my clothes fit right. It was the era of shifts and A-line dresses that were supposed to fit loosely. By the time spring came, I wore my shapeless, black, crepe-thin, dress-length overcoat when out in public, even at meals. I was ashamed of my now ill-fitted clothes.

I had never purchased "store-bought" clothes in Central America. Seamstresses and tailors made clothing by measuring and looking at pictures. Though I didn't have a budget for clothes shopping anyway, I also never considered going to a store in the little town of Toccoa—a long hike from the school. In fact, I rarely visited the town and only to shop at the drugstore.

I went home to El Salvador for summer vacation, sewed new clothes, and returned as a sophomore. My new clothes fit now, but what to do with the food issue?

To help pay for tuition, I waited on tables in the cafeteria for all three meals, every day. I was around food constantly, and I did not want to end up like the year before. I asked God, "What do I do?" and then listened intently. I knew He always heard me, but I didn't know that He would care to answer such a frivolous request.

But I had a distinct impression that His response was simply, "Thank me."

I pondered God's answer. What could I be thankful for? There was only one thought that crossed my mind. God must be training me—but for what? I tried to figure it out. I thought: maybe when I was an old woman, I would need the discipline of staying healthy. It probably would be harder to form good habits later on.

So when I was tempted to eat something I wasn't hungry for or didn't need, I would thank Him for reminding me I was in training. Any time I became worried about weight gain and how that would affect my wardrobe (and image), I moved my focus off of myself and thanked God for offering me discipline.

Now, as an "older woman" of sixty-six, I am so

touched by God's kindness to train me when I was young. He used my insecurity about fitting into a new culture and my fear of not meeting some standard of appearance, to teach me discipline. And not just discipline for physical health but also for spiritual health. I had given Him permission to train me in self-control: an inner strength formed by Him, not by my strength of will-power.

It wasn't until two decades later that I could put all of this into words. Obedience is powerful. Gratitude is an act of faith and trust. Gratitude is an action I can choose, regardless of the circumstance. Gratitude is not only the best and easiest route to focus on God, it turned out to be the only route that actually worked for me long term. Gratitude is the starting point for hope and joy.

I can't change myself. I can't force myself to feel "ok" when my heart is in pain or my mind is confused or my whole being is frozen in fear. But I can choose to receive God's goodness and unimaginable tenderness and love right there in the struggle. His higher reality trumps my earthly reality. Gratitude opened the door to trust Him and hope in Him and find joy in Him.

BLESSINGS FROM THE OLD TESTAMENT

After my four years of high school at Toccoa Falls, I entered Toccoa Falls College, which was situated on the same campus as the high school. That first semester, I was assigned to a freshman roommate, Ellen (not her real name), who could not attend classes very often because of a debilitating illness.

Ellen needed mostly emotional support, but many days she was also unable to leave her bed. I would bring her meals, and I spent many hours mostly listening in conversation. But I felt like I couldn't truly be helpful to her.

I had lived away from home for every school year since second grade. That meant I had grown up fast. I had become a friend and "counselor" to many classmates who had never lived away from home and/or who were going through hardships. But in this case, I couldn't seem to really help this sweet, hurting human being.

Our dorm room was not much bigger than a walk-in closet, accommodating just a bunk bed and a small table with one chair. There was no privacy. But right across the hallway was what I dubbed my "Prayer Closet," a tinier, closet-size room with a window. It was usually vacant, and I spent a lot of time there alone with God. I cried out for answers—for my roommate and myself. I recognized I didn't have the grace to carry Ellen's burden, nor did the other students.

Increasingly, I needed complete alone-time, which I did not find in my room. Every wakeful minute—and even as I was trying to fall asleep—Ellen wanted to talk, out of pure loneliness. But I don't think she could really accept my encouragement. I practiced being grateful in that semester, battling a growing resentment with my living arrangements and my failure to improve them. I knew I couldn't indulge in self-pity; my situation did not compare to what Ellen was going through.

I felt increasingly drawn to my "Prayer Closet," where I listened to the voice of God and began discovering a God who listened to me and comforted me. After my freshman year ended, I knew I needed a change. Long story short, I did not return to Toccoa Falls the following year. I moved out west to attend Multnomah University in Portland, Oregon, my Dad's alma mater.

Some of the most important changes in my life came about as a result of conflict or difficulty. It was a huge transition for me to go off alone to another boarding school on the other side of the US, once again a complete stranger. But it is there I met Garris, the man I fell in love with and married.

The Old Testament is full of stories of difficulty and struggle—and overcoming. Like those who have gone before us, we can choose to put our confidence—our hope—in God. He will produce His joy in us, often at the most surprising times, out of the very backdrop of our struggles.

PART I:
BLESSINGS FROM GENESIS, EXODUS, NUMBERS, JUDGES, II SAMUEL, II KINGS & I CHRONICLES

Blessing of Inheritance
Genesis 18:18-19

*Even if your family inheritance was lost long ago and
your family heritage is in shambles, God's plan has never
changed for you. He is waiting for you to discover your
family mantle and pass it on to your spiritual sons and
daughters. It is your family's legacy, but it is much bigger
than your bloodline—just like Abraham's legacy. All
those of faith are Abraham's children (Galatians 3:7-9).
Through Abraham, all the nations would be blessed.*

In the name of Jesus Christ,
    I bless your spirit with the influence,
    favor, and spiritual authority
    imparted through your family lineage.
May you extend your family mantle
    to successive generations.

I bless you with grace to discover,
    and continue your inheritance—
    your legacy of faith.
The power of these priceless blessings—
    your covenant calling,
    your particular spiritual gifts,
    and your personal assignments—
    are highly significant.

Honor the victories already won in your family line;
    embrace the gifts and talents placed
    on each person, and recognize
    God's unique grace upon your home—
    the strengths, the knowledge, the wisdom,
    and the anointing to fulfill your mission
    and your assignment.

I bless you with a great and lasting legacy
    as you follow closely after God:
    growing in intimate friendship,
    fulfilling your contribution for His Kingdom,
    imparting His heart to future generations—
    expanding and growing,
    birthing many spiritual sons and daughters.

Blessing of Generosity
Genesis 28:10-22; Joshua 1:5; Psalm 27:1; 118:6-7

Jacob was in the third generation that received promises from the Abrahamic covenant. At the point of his greatest struggle, Jacob encountered God in a dream. God extended His grace to Jacob, assuring him that He was the Lord of the past and future. God's promise to Abraham was then made available to Jacob; He would never leave or forsake him.

With deep gratitude, Jacob recognized the Source of goodness. He took hold of the promise and declared that the Lord would be his God. He followed his declaration with an action by giving a tenth of everything back to God—an amount originating with the Abrahamic covenant of grace long before the Mosaic Law.

Jacob knew that everything he had was a gift from God. Generosity is a form of gratitude. Generosity and happiness are even linked neurologically; you feel good when you give. You are wired to be generous, but you must cultivate that generosity.

In the name of Jesus Christ,
    I bless your spirit
    with fearless living
    and with a generosity of spirit.

You may have lost your legacy
    and have no hope of inheritance,
    you may have no safe path home,
    you may be in jeopardy of losing all—
    but listen to God's word:

    I will never leave you alone—not ever.

I will never desert you.
I will never let you down.
I will not loosen my grip on your life.

When you feel alone and helpless,
    take hold of God's promise to be with you,
    to never leave you.

I bless you with Heavenly encounters
    and the reality of God's presence—
    even in the night watches,
    in your dreams.
Like Jacob—may you be able to declare:

    Surely the Lord is in this place.
    I did not know it before—
    I could not see any help on the way.
    I did not know where to turn—
    I was out of options,
    I was in danger of losing everything,
    but now I know the Lord is here.

The place of your greatest vulnerability
    is the place God wants to meet you.
It is the place designed for glory—
    a portal of Heaven.

Rename that place God's Dwelling;
    it is now your place of worship.
Be blessed with seeing into the invisible,
    with seeing angels
    carrying out God-assignments,
    with hearing promises for your future—
    the restoration of your inheritance.

God is with you—He stands by you

and protects you,
He will never leave you alone—not ever,
He will never let you down,
He will not loosen His grip on you,
He provides for you on your journey—
He is your God!

I bless you with dedication to Him—
    a memorial to His goodness.
Worship Him with all your heart,
    with gratitude and generosity.
Give back to Him
    what He has generously given you.

Blessing of Presence
Exodus 33:14-23 & 34:6; Isaiah 11:2; Numbers 11:25

In the name of Jesus Christ,
    I bless your spirit
    with the immense goodness
    of His presence.
God knows you well;
    He knows you by name—
    He has given you His favor,
    He will reveal His presence to you,
    He will make His goodness visible to you,
    He will go with you to the end of your journey,
    He covers you with His hand for safety,
    and He will give you rest.

Be blessed with His glory—
    His manifest presence.
Listen and receive His proclamation:

    I am compassionate and gracious to you,
    I am endlessly patient with you,
    I am loyal in love—so deeply true to you—
    and to the generations after you.

May you be overwhelmed with worship;
    confess any deviation
    from who you were created to be,
    confess your propensity to rebel—
    holding God off at a distance.

Confess your fear
    to trust His goodness toward you,
    and refuse to move ahead on your own,

without His guiding presence.
I bless you with desire to be led by Him.

Just as the Spirit of God rests upon the Messiah,
the Spirit of God rests upon you:
the Spirit of wisdom and understanding,
the Spirit of counsel and might,
the Spirit of knowledge.

The Rest-Giver rests upon you;
be blessed with rest in His presence,
be blessed with soothing quiet and stillness.
I bless you with security and peace.

Blessing of Your Promised Land
Numbers 14:6-9

"Hear and obey" the word of the Lord. The fear, unbelief, and resulting disobedience of the ten spies caused a rebellion among the Israelites to the point that they planned to stone Joshua and Caleb to death. Evil reports can produce death in many forms. Instead, identify unbelief as the trap it is, and enter the land given to you, despite the giants. God promised you a land flowing with abundance—He did not promise you it would be "giant-free."

In the name of Jesus Christ,
    I bless your spirit with belief.
I bless you with clear direction from God
    and the willingness to take risk—
    stepping out in obedience to His word
    and advancing.

When the enemy of your soul
    is too big and you are at a disadvantage,
    when you feel restricted by economy or health,
    when you lack training
    or feel less capable than others,
    when you are fearful to the point of panic,
    don't stay in the wilderness any longer—
    believe God's promise.

When God commissions you to do something
    bigger than yourself, something far greater
    than your abilities and gifting,
    something way beyond your wisdom
    and discernment,
    may you agree with God—

declare that He is big enough.
Exchange all of your abilities for His,
    receive His help,
    take Him at His word—
    take hold of His promise.

When the enemy opposes you
    and stands between you and your promise,
    declare God's higher reality—
    with the breath of His word,
    He draws from the invisible realm
    and creates visible worlds.
What He has promised is already yours,
    reserved for you in Heaven—
    what He has asked of you,
    He will confirm and perform
    and reveal on earth.

I bless you with belief and obedience;
    you can trust what God tells you to do,
    no matter how impossible.

Make this your declaration:

> *God, you are pleased to give me*
> *this exceedingly good land—*
> *a land filled with abundance.*
> *I am fully able to overtake my enemies.*
> *Lord, you are with me—you are on my side—*
> *I don't have to be afraid.*

Where God has called you to journey,
    He has anointed you to overcome:
    He is the one who gave you the promise.
He is more passionate about you receiving
    your promise than you are.

If you are stretched beyond your limitations
    and have lost your self-confidence,
    then you are now dependent on God
    and already experiencing breakthrough.

I bless you with exponential increase
    in your belief that God is true to His word.
I bless you with continued acquisition
    of your promised land
    at every step you take.
I bless you with abundance.

Blessing of Simple Faith
Numbers 21:4-9; Hebrews 11:1 & 12:2; John 3:7 & 14-15

I read A. W. Tozer's books in high school, and they changed my whole paradigm of faith. In his book, The Pursuit of God, *I read about faith in its profound simplicity. It was actually achievable. As I wrote this blessing, I was struck with just how much this one truth has impacted my perspective on life.*

Jesus helps Nicodemus understand faith by explaining Israel's journey through the wilderness to the Promised Land. The people's hard hearts of cynicism produced constant complaining to such a degree that their words opened a door of death. Their presumptions invited judgment; the plague of poisonous snakes was a self-inflicted punishment.

In order to stop the carnage, God instructed Moses to fashion a serpent out of brass and hang it up on a pole. The simple act of "looking" at it would be their deliverance. Under the Old Covenant, the physical act of "looking" at the pole and brass serpent (representing sin and death) is synonymous with "believing" in the New Covenant Christ—the Messiah.

The pole was a prophetic symbol of the future Cross. Jesus would hang on a tree; He was "made sin." An innocent man bore the full guilt of all humanity's rebellion and resulting evil (chaos, trouble, sorrow). The enemy would be defeated and death would be conquered. Salvation is given to all who believe in Jesus by "looking" to Him with the eyes of our spirit.

In the name of Jesus Christ,
    I bless your spirit with faith's simplicity.
Faith is made possible for you as a gift from God;

it is the only way to approach God,
it is the only way to receive forgiveness,
deliverance, salvation, and communion—
it is a spiritual rebirth.

I bless you with a child-like faith—
a simple faith, a heart of trust and dependency.
Believing in Jesus Christ is *looking* to Him,
the author and finisher of your faith.

Keep your spirit's gaze on Him;
even when you don't believe, look at Him.
Look at Him always—
in your best and worst moments,
in your strongest and weakest moments.

Faith in its simplicity is an internal act;
it needs no external force,
no special event or place,
no special person or thing.

If you pull away or leave Jesus,
you will always be dissatisfied,
you will always long for Him.
I bless you with a single-hearted focus on Him—
a liberated heart to commit fully to Him,
to follow after Him, to walk and talk with Him,
to dream and plan with Him,
to live life with Him.

Blessing of Encounter
Judges 6:1-8:28

God raised up Gideon to lead an army to save Israel from the Midianites. These invaders were so numerous, and their devastation for seven years so extensive, that they were compared to swarms of locusts.

At first Gideon argued with God, saying that he was too poor to be called to such an important, impossible task; he was from the poorest clan in his region, and he was the poorest one in all his clan. But when he experienced a face-to-face encounter with the Angel of the Lord, he built an alter, calling it, "The-Lord-Is-Peace." Gideon then proceeded to obey God, winning an astounding, miraculous victory for Israel. Afterward, there was peace in the land.

In the name of Jesus Christ,
　　I bless you with deliverance
　　from your enemy's assaults.

Have you found yourself thinking:

> *If God is with me,*
> *why has all this happened to me?*
> *Where are all the miracles*
> *and wonders I've heard about?*
> *Didn't God deliver them?*
> *I've not seen a miraculous intervention —*
> *God must not want to bless me.*

I bless you with a face-to-face
　　encounter with the Lord.
Hear His words of proclamation:

I am with you, mighty warrior!
Go in this might of yours;
deliver your people and land
from the enemy.
Have I not sent you?
Do not fear—you will not die.

Respond to His word, however improbable
    or seemingly impossible.
Your success is measured
    by doing things God's way,
    not by what you accomplish.

Even when you feel forsaken,
    when you are the weakest
    and most impoverished of all,
    I bless you with the word of the Lord
    and His assessment of you.

By simple obedience to His instructions,
    He will act on your behalf.
When He acts, everything changes.
He will be free to make a way for you—
    He will establish you,
    He will impart might, valor, courage,
    true humility, and faith to you.

Be led under His anointing—
    go when He calls you,
    depend upon Him at every turn,
    follow His every instruction,
    and give Him the glory—
    before and after your victory.

When you fulfill God's assignment,
    don't establish a dynasty for yourself,

don't erect a memorial to your victory—
give others credit, even when it belongs to you.

I bless you, your family, your descendants,
your tribe, and your land
with God's might and supernatural strength
to deliver you and protect you.

I bless you with wholeness, security,
well-being and prosperity.
May you encounter Peace Himself;
may peace be with you.

Blessing of Royalty
2 Samuel 9:1-13; Ephesians 2:10

Prince Mephibosheth—Jonathan's son and the grandson of King Saul—was completely unaware of his inheritance. Though born of royalty, he grew up in the wilderness with no sense of his true destiny or calling. When presented to King David and restored to his true inheritance, he shuffled and stammered, "Who am I that you pay attention to a stray dog like me?"

I bless your spirit,
 in the name of Jesus Christ,
 with the reality of your heritage.
You were created in the joy of the Trinity;
 by His Hand you were
 intricately formed and cradled
 in your mother's womb.
You were born royalty—God's child.

Before you were born,
 God planned your destiny.
In advance He planned for your good—
 to give you a future of goodness.
He claimed you as His own,
 to give you a royal inheritance.
He planned for the good works you will do
 to fulfill your destiny.

God knew full well the conditions, the affairs,
 and the state of this world
 that you were born into.
He knew the choices, the schemes
 and plans of humanity.
He knew your fierce and cruel enemy—

He knew and planned for your deliverance,
to raise you up to your full inheritance:
to walk in the King's authority and power.

Your season of shame—
your belief that you are worthless—
that season is over.
Though you were cheated of your inheritance,
I bless you with full restoration
of your royal rights and privileges.
Take your place at the King's table.

Blessing of the Invisible Realm
II Kings 6:8-23; Zechariah 2:5

Bless each other for increase in spiritual sight. Elisha prayed that his servant would have sight into the invisible realm. Until his eyes were opened, the servant could only see the enemy—a great army from the raiding bands of Aram—surrounding them. In reality, they were surrounded by a much greater army of angels.

Elisha captured this great army by praying that God would strike their eyes with blindness. The prophet then led them, blinded, into Samaria, where he prayed that their eyes be opened. The army found themselves surrounded and helpless. Elisha instructed the King to not kill them, but to feed them. Blessing them first with a feast, Elisha then sent them home. Those armies never entered the land of Israel again.

In the name of Jesus Christ,
    I bless your spirit with vision—
    believe what seems impossible
    by *seeing* the invisible;
    see beyond the natural realm
    to what God is doing,
    and see your incredible safety!

Pray for others to see what you see.
Elisha prayed:

    Don't be afraid,
    for those who are with us are more
    than those who are with them.
    God, I pray, open his eyes that he may see.

You are surrounded by angelic

warriors of light—ringed by fire,
and God is the glory in your midst,
ever present with you.

No matter how great the opposition—
how subtle and deceptive,
how fierce and destructive,
there is more protection on your side
than on their side.
There is more for you and with you
than against you.

I bless you with words of knowledge
to give warning of the enemy's plans:
to watch out for traps,
to warn others of ambushes,
to thwart secrets whispered in the dark.

I bless you with great favor
to influence leaders, decision makers,
and those who govern.
I bless you with the ability to discern trouble
and life-threatening issues
and the ability to offer God's unique solutions
and facilitate His plans.

Pray that God would blind the eyes
of those who seek to harm you and yours.
Pray that God would abort their plan of attack.
Pray that their eyes would be opened
to encounter the one true God.

By your acts of mercy, your blessing,
and your release,
they will also see God's mercy
and salvation.

May you experience peace with those
    who came against you.
I bless you with peace—
    never to be attacked by them again!

I bless you with authority to impart vision
    and help others see what you see:
    the secrets of the Kingdom of Heaven on earth.

Blessing of Knowledge
I Chronicles 12:32; Isaiah 11:1-3

The sons of Issachar had knowledge of the times; they knew what Israel needed to do.

In the name of Jesus Christ,
    I bless your spirit with understanding
    for the times you are in,
    and with the knowledge of what to do.

I bless you with Holy Spirit vision
    to see what God is doing—
    what He is preparing in the invisible.
I bless you with wisdom
    as signs begin to manifest on the earth.

I bless you with knowledge of what to do
    in each change and shift of season.
The life-giving Spirit of God
    will hover over you,
    imparting wisdom and skill to live rightly,
    and inspiring craftsmanship
    to display His glory.

Instead of judging by the natural world—
    what your eye sees or what your ear hears—
    receive knowledge and direction
    from the Spirit of Wisdom.
May you release supernatural clarity of vision.

PART II:
BLESSINGS FROM THE
BOOK OF PSALMS

Blessing of Laughter
Psalm 2:1-4; Psalm 37:12-13; John 17:1-26

*Psalm 2:1-12 is a messianic psalm that applies to Jesus
Christ and is mentioned five times in the New Testament.
I love that God's response to rebellion is to laugh—and
then give His solution. He tells His Son to ask for those
nations as His inheritance. Jesus, in turn, will tell us to
ask for the nations as our inheritance. I started imagining
how God is answering all of our requests!*

In the name of Jesus Christ,
    I bless your spirit with laughter
    in the Holy Spirit.
Many blessings are waiting for you
    because you have taken refuge in God.

Though the nations plan a rebellion
    against the Lord Most High—
    coming together and breaking away
    from the Creator God and His Christ—
    their plots are futile.

The enthroned God merely laughs at them;
    then, in righteous anger,
    He settles the issue.
Hear the decree of God to His Son:

    You are my Son.
    As your Father,
    ask me to give you the nations,
    and I will do it.
    They will become your legacy.

Jesus, the Anointed One

has asked for the nations
and now He says to you:

Ask me to give you the nations,
and I will do it.
They will become your legacy.

In response to the Messiah's invitation,
here is my prayer:

As you requested, Jesus:
I ask you for the nations of this world
to become my legacy.
I ask for an outpouring of revival
in our families and in your Church.
I ask for a double rain of your Spirit.
I ask for transformation of hearts.
I ask for a billion salvations
and a reformation of the cultures.
I ask that you be made famous
in the whole world!

Blessing of Rest
Psalm 3

David the Psalmist wrote this song when forced to flee from his son, Absalom. You can break any word curses that have been spoken to you, or that you have spoken against yourself. They will no longer have power over you.

I bless your spirit, soul, and body
    with safety and rest,
    in the name of Jesus Christ.
May you know—truly know,
    in the deepest parts of your heart—
    that you are blessed with the shield
    of the Lord round about you.
He is your dwelling place,
    He has surrounded you with Himself,
    He *is* your shield.

When you are surrounded by enemies—
    when there are so many against you
    that even your own family fights you
    and whispers behind your back:

You are hopeless.
Even God can't deliver you this time.

I bless you with this declaration
by the Psalmist, David:

Lord, in the depth of my heart,
I truly know that you are my Shield.
You surround me.
You are my dwelling place.

You are the only One
who restores my courage.
You continually cover me
with your glory.
You lift my head high
when I am bowed in shame.

You send me your fathering help,
so now I can lie down and sleep.
I will wake up in safety
because I am surrounded by you—
in your glory.

Dark powers have come against me,
but I won't be afraid.
I cry out to you—
come and save me, Lord!
Salvation belongs to you:
you alone are my Deliverer,
you are the true Hero.
You will rescue me.
Your blessing of favor is upon me.

When dark powers prepare to devour you—
    their words like sharpened weapons
    of destruction—don't be afraid!
Cry out to God for help and deliverance
    and get ready for rescue:
    He will break any dark curse
    spoken against you.

Speak in the name of Jesus Christ,
    who has all power and authority:

I break the power of this word curse:

that I am hopeless,
that even God can't deliver me.

God, you are just and merciful,
and your mercy triumphs over judgment.
I too extend mercy
rather than punishment.
I bless my enemies with deliverance
and an encounter with you, God.

I renounce any authority
given to the enemy—
spirit, soul and body—
making this word curse null and void—
no longer having any power to harm me.

Salvation belongs to you, Jesus:
You alone are my Deliverer.
You are the true Hero—
You will rescue me.
Your blessing of favor is upon me.

Blessing of Treasure
Psalm 18:16-29

In the name of Jesus Christ,
    I bless you with this treasure:
    every surrender to God
    turns into a blessing.
He brings Heaven's deliverance
    to the humble.
Because you kept your integrity
    by surrendering to Him,
    He came down into your darkness
    to rescue you.

At your weakest point,
    you are blessed with God's love
    breaking open a way for you.
He takes you out of your calamity,
    your depth of despair,
    your trouble and helplessness
    at the hands of your enemy,
    and draws you to Himself.

At your most vulnerable,
    He holds on to you,
    He rescues you,
    and He brings you into a beautiful,
    wide-open space.
He saves you because He delights in you.

You are blessed when you live in the light,
    keeping your heart clean,
    following God no matter what,
    listening for His words,
    obeying His requests.

You are rewarded with a close friendship
    and oneness of heart with Him.

With shrewdness and cunning,
    God outwits the devious.
The proud He disregards,
    but to the humble
    He loves to prove His loyalty,
    His purity, His goodness,
    His mercy, His truth.

I bless you with a floodlight of hope;
    He is your revelation light!
All at once, He will enlighten your darkness.
In His brightness, you can see the path ahead.

I bless you with supernatural powers.
With God's strength and blazing glory,
    you will crush an enemy horde,
    you will leap over walls,
    you will vault the highest fences,
    advancing through every stronghold.

God is your treasure—live in the richness of Him.

Blessing of a Warrior
Psalm 18:30-36 & 50

In the name of Jesus Christ,
    I bless your spirit
    with the power of overcoming.

God's path for you is perfect—
    all His promises prove true.
You are wrapped in His power,
    you are armed with His grace,
    and stationed in his love.

He makes your feet like hind's feet
    to ascend the highest peaks of His glory
    and stand in heavenly places.

I bless you with a warrior spirit
    when you descend into battle.
You are shielded by His presence—
    secured and strengthened,
    empowered to conquer your enemy.

God has cleared the ground;
    your footing is secure,
    and you can rise above the chaos
    and scale the heights of the Spirit.

He has armed you for battle—
    training you to not back down or turn back,
    training you to pin down your enemy
    and conquer darkness.

I bless you with victory on every side,
    time and time again!

Blessing of God's Silent Story
Psalm 19:1-6

Over the course of his life, David the Psalmist often lived with only the heavens as a roof over his head. Whether you are living without a shelter, in dire circumstances, or just looking up to the skies in a moment of reflection, I bless you with a download from Heaven.

In the name of Jesus Christ,
    I bless your spirit
    with deep revelations of God
    in the mystical wonders of creation.

Look up and take in the profound
    majesty of the heavens.
Their expanse gives you a message without words,
    declaring the work of God's hands,
    revealing knowledge of your Creator.

Through the mysteries of the heavens,
    space itself speaks His story
    across the wide horizon.

The heavens are always rehearsing
    the glory of God, displaying His splendor,
    writing His story in the stars,
    prophesying His plan.

I bless you with heart-catching glimpses
    of your Creator-God as you look up.
I bless you with receptivity to the Good News
    clearly spelled across the skies,
    so that all may know the Messiah
    and come to Him.

Blessing of Treasuring His Word
Psalm 19:7-14

In the name of Jesus Christ,
    I bless your spirit with shining radiance
    from the light of His perfect Word—
    the Word that revives and restores your soul,
    the Word that makes you whole.

I bless you with God's powerful teachings
    that lead you to truth,
    that change you,
    that make you wise.

His Word will fill you with joy and cheer.
His Word will challenge you.
His Word will rearrange your world.

I bless you with the revelation light
    of God's Word.
As you treasure His Word,
    you will receive His treasures.

Blessing of Miraculous Deliverance
Psalm 20:1-9

The phrase "may God give you success" is another way of saying, "I bless you with success."

In the name of Jesus Christ,
> be delivered in your day of danger;
> may your safety be secured,
> may the God of Grace save you.

Be blessed with answered prayer:
> may God carry out your every plan,
> may He give you every desire of your heart,
> may He give you success.

Some use their own weapons
> and wisdom to find strength,
> but may you boast in the Lord, your God,
> who makes you strong
> and who gives you victory.

Your miraculous deliverance
> can only be won by God.
Through His saving strength
> and by His mighty hand,
> be blessed with outpourings of miracles.

You will rise up full of courage,
> and your enemies will not prevail—
> they will collapse in defeat.
I bless you with victory, with celebration,
> with flying flags and shouts of joy.

On the day you call on your King,
    may He give you His answer
    and His winning hand of victory!

Blessing of Confidence
Psalm 27; 118:6

In the name of Jesus Christ,
    I bless your spirit with confidence—
    He is your light and salvation.
He is on your side, He is your defense;
    so who would you be afraid of
    or what would you live in dread of?

I bless you with such great confidence
    that you can declare like the Psalmist:

> *I know the Lord is for me.*
> *I will never be afraid*
> *of what people may do to me.*
> *God is there ready to help me.*

When your enemies want to devour you,
    when bullies and tough guys try to harm you,
    or war breaks out all around you,
    I bless you with Spirit-inspired confidence.

Even if your family and friends have forsaken you,
    remember—God is your help;
    He will not abandon you or forsake you.
In the day of your trouble,
    He will conceal you and surround you,
    He will lift you up
    and plant your feet on solid ground.

Do you hear God whisper, *Seek me?*
Respond with, *Yes, I will seek you.*
He is not hiding from you,
    He is not angry at you,

He is right there beside you—
He is your help.

Wait for Him—stay with Him,
    meditate on His word,
    be strong and take heart.
Don't quit—you will not despair
    because you believed you would see
    the goodness of the Lord on the earth—
    and in your life.
Be confident that you will encounter
    the beauty of the Lord
    as you dwell in His presence.

Blessing of Refreshment
Psalm 36:1-10

In the name of Jesus Christ,
    I bless your spirit
    with His limitless, exquisite love,
    with His mercy that reaches higher
    than the highest heavens,
    with His infinite faithfulness,
    with His kindness and tender care,
    with His unmovable righteousness,
    and His verdicts full of wisdom.

In His largeness, you will not get lost—
    nothing slips through the cracks,
    nothing is forgotten—
    not you, not even a sparrow.

Even when rebellion runs rampant,
    you can find a hiding place
    in the shadow of God's wings.
When wisdom and goodness
    are forgotten and forsaken
    and there is no awe of God,
    I bless you with Love's influence
    to thwart evil.

God is the Flowing Fountain—
    a cascading light of life.
All may drink of His anointing;
    drink from the river of His delights,
    drink with pleasure from His pure springs,
    drink your fill—drink in His life
    springing up to refresh you—to satisfy you.

In your nearness to Him,
    you can more easily receive
    His favor upon you.
I declare a flow of more blessings—
    an outpouring of His blessings.

Blessing of Uncontainable Joy
Psalm 92:1-8

I wrote this blessing for a prophetic pastor who has led worship for years. So much life and truth and healing and joy have flowed from his ministry of worship.

In the name of Jesus Christ,
    I bless your spirit with uncontainable,
    overflowing gladness—
    gladness spilling out from your heart
    with shouts of joy
    for all that God has done.

I bless you with a heart of gratitude
    for His kindness and love
    at each and every sunrise.
I bless you with songs celebrating
    His faithful presence through the night.

I bless you with the sounds of Heaven—
    with melodies of praise,
    with each musical instrument
    joined to your heart—
    overflowing with worship,
    with thankfulness,
    with proclamations,
    with declarations of God's goodness.

I bless you with stories of miracles
    at work in you and around you.
May you discover His deep, glorious secrets
    saturating everything He does—discover
    His depth of purpose in all His ways.

As you experience the blessing
of celebrating the One who is
the source of your joy,
I bless you with uncontainable joy.

Blessing of Old Age
Psalm 92:10-15

In the name of Jesus Christ,
    I bless your spirit with the fresh oil
    of His anointing:
    He has empowered your life for triumph,
    He will make you strong and mighty.

God transplanted you
    into the Kingdom of light,
    into His heavenly realm.
You are immortal and immovable.

As a lover of God,
    you have been made to flourish—
    growing in victory,
    standing with strength.

I bless you into your old age,
    as you thrive in His presence—
    overflowing with anointing—
    with more compassion and joy,
    more peace and kindness,
    more patience and loyalty,
    more inner strength and faithfulness.

May you proclaim with pleasure:

    God, you are so good!
    You are my beautiful strength.
    You never made a mistake with me!

Blessing of Beauty
Psalm 93:1-5

Holiness is the beauty that fills God's house.
May His beauty of holiness
    fill your spirit, soul, and body,
    your house, and your family—
    in the name of Jesus Christ.

Eternity is God's home—
    He sits securely on His throne,
    regal power surrounds Him,
    His royal decrees will never change—
    they will last forever.

When chaos challenges you,
    remember the mighty power
    and surging strength of God.
He is sovereign over all.
He knows what He is doing:
    hear the sound of His voice—
    listen to Him silence the enemy.

God is full of majesty and strength—
    He is the One who abides forevermore.
You are profoundly blessed with the beauty
    of His majesty and holiness.

Blessing of Goodness
Psalm 119:68

Everything God does
    is beautiful and good;
    everything God does
    flows from His goodness.
In the name of Jesus Christ,
    I bless your spirit
    with declarations of His goodness.

Regardless of any evil around you,
    settle it in your heart once and for all
    that God is good all the time,
    and you can trust Him.
I bless you with the power of His goodness.

The words God speaks to you
    are worth more than all the riches
    and wealth in the whole world.
I bless you with dwelling
    in the wealth of His goodness.

Blessing of Safety in Surrender
Psalm 141; Galatians 6:6-10

In the name of Jesus Christ,
    I bless your spirit with safeguards.
Ask Him for sensitivity to recognize temptation—
    careful of the company you keep.
Ask Him to deliver you from evil.

Speak the reality of your safety in Him.
Your words carry great power:
    the power of life and death—
    choose life!

I bless you with humility to receive
    godly correction without offense—
    accepting it like an honor
    you cannot refuse.
It will be like healing medicine.

If others are mistaken about you,
    your words will be proven true.
I bless you with grace to surrender
    any judgment or punishment.
Cause and effect, planting and reaping—
    these physical and spiritual laws are in full force.
What you plant, you will harvest—
    whether or not it is yet visible to others.

I bless you with speaking life-giving words:
    Be safe in Him—no longer defenseless
    but protected in your surrender.
Partner with the victory that is already yours.

Blessing of Hope
Psalm 142

This was David's prayer when he was hiding from Solomon in a cave.

In the name of Jesus Christ,
    I bless you with hope in God—
    your only certainty.
I bless you with hope when you are low
    and in desperate need—
    when no one takes notice of you,
    when you cannot escape trouble,
    when no one cares.
I bless you with shelter in the Hiding Place—
    in the only hope you have.

Cry out to God—go ahead,
    spill out your heart to Him,
    tell Him your troubles,
    tell Him your desperation.
When you are overwhelmed
    and ready to give up,
    when you are no match
    for those who persecute you,
    when you are in need of rescue
    from the traps of the enemy,
    God is your help and hope.

I bless you with stories of deliverance
    to celebrate all the wonderful things
    God has done for you!

Blessing of Great Mercy
Psalm 145:1-19

God did not force the Israelites to love Him or follow Him.
When they made wrong choices, He did not bring disaster
upon them; disaster was the consequence of their choices
apart from His protection. Even though Israel kept
choosing the path to disaster, God kept delivering them
when they turned back to Him. King David's poetic song
describes this merciful heart of God.

In the name of Jesus Christ,
> I bless your spirit with explosive praise
> for the mighty mercy of God.

I bless you with discovering more of His glory,
> more of His magnificent splendor,
> more of His mighty, wondrous acts—
> His awesome acts of power,
> His eternal excellence.

As God's goodness and beauty
> bring bliss to your heart,
> celebrate and thank Him!
I bless you with ecstatic joy in His kindness
> when you didn't deserve it—
> in His patience when you failed Him.

He is faithful to fulfill every promise He made.
He sustains you when you are weak and feeble,
> He lifts you up when you are bent with burdens,
> He gives you what you hunger for,
> He satisfies your longings.

God is fair and righteous in everything He does—

His every action is wrapped in love.
He draws near when you call out to Him,
    He listens closely to you—
    hearing what your heart really longs for—
    and He brings you His saving strength.
You will receive even more
    than what you ask for.

Tell the world of His limitless power,
    His glorious majesty,
    His constant goodness,
    and His great mercy.

To believe in the goodness of God
    is to experience mercy;
    is to see and know Him.

PART III:
BLESSINGS FROM THE BOOK OF ISAIAH

Through the prophet Isaiah, God communicated His desire and plan to turn people away from disaster and to lay a foundation of hope and promise. Through Israel, He desired to lead all nations out from under judgment to safety and salvation. I've been impacted by the Book of Isaiah since I was a nineteen-year-old college girl; I've read part or all of it every year since then.

A few years ago, my dear friend Lois (Calderwood) Martin gave me a wonderful commentary by J. Alec Motyer called The Prophecy of Isaiah. *While writing these blessings, I referred to Motyer's book for history, context, and an understanding of the rich Hebrew language.*

Blessing of Overwhelming Joy
Isaiah 35:8-10

This prophecy has multifaceted application. Israel experienced release from captivity and a joyful arrival back home. It is also a messianic promise fulfilled in stages by the ministry of Jesus. It is a beautiful, prophetic word describing our release from any type of captivity and our homecoming. We were all prodigals.

In the name of Jesus Christ,
    I bless your spirit
    with the pure joy of your salvation.
God has made a way for you
    called the *Way of Holiness.*

Whoever walks this *Way*
    has chosen to receive
    God's divine provision.
You cannot accidentally wander off:
    the *Way* is clearly marked.

Only those who disqualify themselves
    by not accepting God's saving grace
    cannot travel this Highway.

Jesus, your Kinsman-Redeemer
    is the only one who can intervene
    on your behalf—
    He is the only one who can redeem you.

As your next-of-kin, He has the right
    to take your needs as His own:
    a right which no one dares usurp,
    a right He gladly shoulders on your behalf.

I bless you with shouts of gladness
     all along the way.
Jesus journeys with you,
     carrying all your needs and cares.

As you reach your destination,
     sorrow and sighing
     transform into unbreakable joy.

Blessing of the One Who Remembers You
Isaiah 40:21-27; I Kings 8:27

Israel has always possessed the knowledge of God. I was particularly struck by God's faithfulness to them and to us, considering what has been revealed to us for so long. His desire is for us — and to reach others through us.

In the name of Jesus Christ,
    I bless your spirit
    with an awakening.

Have you not heard?
Do you not know?
Have you not discerned who God is?
Listen to His words:

> *Who is like me?*
> *Lift up your eyes to the night skies.*
> *Who made all this?*
> *Who has created the multitude of stars —*
> *revealing them by night,*
> *counting each one,*
> *calling them all by name,*
> *never overlooking a single one?*
> *I did — by the greatness of my might*
> *and the strength of my power.*
>
> *Why would you ever say*
> *I lost track of you,*
> *I don't care what happens to you,*
> *I don't see the injustice you have suffered?*

Are you asking:
    Does God know what I'm going through?
    How can God allow what is happening?
    Is my problem too insignificant?
    Has God changed His mind about me?
    Does He really care?
    Why are my prayers not answered?

Why would you ever say
    He has lost track of you,
    or that He doesn't care what happens to you,
    or that He doesn't see your suffering?
He never overlooks a star in the sky—
    how much more does He care about you?

You have been told the truth.
I bless you with relearning
    what you already know;
    I bless you with an acceptance
    to the truth you already possess.

As Creator, God has all glory and power.
He is transcendent, eternal, untiring.
He posses unfathomable wisdom—
    you never need to doubt His capacity,
    you never will understand all His ways.

Nothing compares to God:
    He is all power, all wisdom,
    all dignity, all sovereignty,
    all authority.
He is above comparison.

He is a Holy God,
    with unattainable, moral perfection.
He is the enthroned God

with the whole universe as His "tent."
Earth cannot contain Him—
    even the highest Heaven
    cannot contain Him.

The stars, innumerable though they may be,
    exist and are in place only by God's will:
    He summons them and directs them,
    He calls them each by name.
    He knows by name every item
    in His complex creation.

He made Heaven and earth;
    He manages the totality
    and the individual aspects of creation.
He made you—how can He forget you?
How can He forget your suffering?
He cares for every facet of you.

I bless you with remembering God's reality!

Blessing of Exuberance
Isaiah 41:14-16

In this passage of Isaiah, God's people face an impossible task. Isaiah uses poetic hyperbole by calling them a "worm" (a picture of human weakness) in comparison to God. A worm can't flatten mountains, but God says He will turn the people into threshing-sledges capable of threshing mountains—an otherwise impossible obstacle. He will then turn them into winnowers that separate the straw from the chaff. Rather than the normal, gentle wind blowing the straw into piles, a gale will remove the chaff (obstacles), leaving no trace of them.

In the name of Jesus Christ,
    I bless your spirit with exuberant joy—
    with entering freely into all
    that He has done for you.

Do not measure any barriers
    in proportion to your ability,
    your intelligence, or your power
    to remove them.
Measure obstacles in proportion
    to what God has done:
    what He has promised to do for you,
    what He has promised to do in you.

I bless you with reassurance
    and confidence.
The Holy One—your Redeemer,
    your Next-of-Kin,
    has taken your needs
    as His own needs.
Hear His declaration to you:

Don't be afraid—
even though the obstacle
is insurmountable for you,
I will help you. I will transform you:
I will prepare you for the task,
I will make you new, efficient,
and in prime condition.

You will pulverize your obstacle,
and by divine power,
it will be removed without a trace.
You will be free to celebrate—
joyful, exuberant, and confident
in what I have done for you.

I bless you with certainty
    of God's promise to help you
    and transform you.
When facing insurmountable obstacles,
    I bless you with divine power.

He will take your inherent weakness
    and transform you;
    He will turn you into a warrior,
    empowered by His word of promise.
He will turn your helplessness
    and hopelessness into certainty
    and confidence;
    He will prepare you for each task.

By the whirlwind of His Spirit,
    He will pulverize your obstacle
    and remove it without a trace.
Be filled and blessed with exuberant joy
    because of what God has done for you.

Blessing of the I Am
Isaiah 43:8-13

Picture a courtroom: one party is the people of Israel who have lost both their sight and hearing of God by constant refusal to see and hear. The other party is an international group who worships false gods and no-gods, yet they are more inspired by their belief in their gods.

The people of Israel are a witness to God's deity as the one true God. They are witnesses of His personal relationship and commitment to them. They have testimonies of God's great care for them in every arena and of His deliverances so that they would not perish (the Exodus was His first act of redemption specifically for Israel). But how can those who are now blind and deaf testify in court? God will have to speak for Himself.

I bless your spirit, in the name of Jesus Christ,
    with declarations of truth concerning
    the great I Am, the one true God
    and His absolute sovereignty:
    His sovereignty over the natural order,
    His sovereignty over people and their affairs,
    His sovereign acts determining
    the course of events.

God proceeds from none
    and is succeeded by none:
    He always has existed,
    He is the one and only God,
    He is the one and only
    Savior and Deliverer.

God acts on your behalf, for your sake:
    His acts reveal the truth about Himself,

His acts write your story—your testimony,
His acts are firm evidence of who He is.

Listen to His words of proclamation:

You are my witness—I picked you
and told you the truth about myself
so that you will believe me,
so that you will know me,
so that you understand who I am,
so that you trust me—
convinced that I Am who I am.

Before me there was no god—
after me there will be no god.
I am God: I am the one
who spoke to you and saved you—
not some strange god among you.
I am the only Savior there is.

I foretold and proclaimed what existed.
I declared these truths about myself.
I am unique, there is no one like me.
You have discerned who I am,
so you are my witness and *evidence.*
I told you these truths about myself
so that you can tell the rest of the world.

Yes, I am God:
I have always been God—from eternity.
I will always be God.
I act and no one can take anything from me;
who can unmake what I make?
Who can reverse it?

I bless you with the truth

of who God is;
He is the One who declares truth
and makes His word heard,
understood, believed, and trusted.

Entrust yourself to the great I Am,
    not by wrestling to understand Him
    but by opening your heart to receive
    the impartation of His words—
    His breath of divine truth.

May you become a mighty witness
    to the cultures of the world—
    evidence of the one true God,
    with powerful testimonies of His
    sovereignty and might,
    with stories of His intervention
    and redemption and His all-
    encompassing care and love.

When He acts, no one
    can take anything from Him.
No one can unmake what He degrees,
    no one can reverse what He declares.

Blessing of the Way-Maker
Isaiah 43:19-21

The "new thing" is Israel's deliverance from captivity.
God not only wanted to bring the Israelites into harmony,
He wanted to bring the whole world into harmony. This
passage also points to God's plans for the day of the
Messiah.

In the name of Jesus Christ,
    I bless your spirit in this new hour.
I bless you with taking hold of something new:
    a fresh, new way you have never been before,
    a fresh plan you have not imagined,
    a fresh, new season you could not envision.

You are birthing His promises.
Hear the Lord's declaration and invitation:

> *Look forward — not back.*
> *I will do a new thing.*
> *It is springing up —*
> *it is bursting out!*
> *Are you aware of it?*
> *Can you see it?*
> *Look — there it is!*
> *I am making a way for you.*
> *I am making a road*
> *through the wilderness,*
> *a river through the desert.*

I bless you with this new day!
Like a seed germinating
    and breaking through the soil,
    your time has come.

God is doing a new thing—
    He is delivering you,
    He is delivering your family
    from the bondage of depression,
    slavery, oppression.

He is bringing you into harmony
    with Himself—transforming you.
All the people and cultures will respond—
    even nature will benefit
    from the harmony created by you and God.

I bless you with a way forward—
    See it. Know it.
    God is your Way-Maker.

Blessing of a Burden-Bearing God
Isaiah 46:1-4

False religion produces mental blindness. This passage in Isaiah is a striking comparison of God and false gods. Bel (Marduk) was the city-god of Babylon and Nebo was Bel's son, the god of writing and wisdom. These statues/idols were brought together and carried in the New Year procession to decree and write down the fates for each coming year.

With Cyrus's conquest, Bel collapsed and Nebo crumpled. In the evacuation, they were loaded up and carried on beasts of burden, themselves now burdensome and wearying even to the animals. These gods who were supposed to rescue in a crisis could not intervene and rescue themselves. God reminded Israel that, unlike these false gods, He has carried them on His shoulder and upheld them from birth.

In the name of Jesus Christ,
    I bless your spirit
    with dependence on the only One
    who rescues you and sustains you.
Jesus Christ is your Burdon-Bearer—
    your existence depends on Him.

I bless you with discernment to recognize
    to whom you have given your allegiance,
    in what you have put your hope.
If you are carrying anything heavy
    and burdensome;
      if your burden is unsustainable—
    collapsing and crumbling

and in need of intervention and rescue—
then you have put your hope
in something other than God.

Hear His amazing words of comfort:

Listen to me—
I carried you from the womb.
I've been carrying you
from the day you were born,
and I will keep carrying you
when you are old—
even to your graying years!

Remember this: I have carried you
and I will keep on carrying you:
I will hold you,
I will sustain you,
I will rescue you.

God won't put anything heavy
or ill-fitting on you,
remember: He carries you—
He's been carrying you from the womb,
and He will carry you into your old age.
I bless you with the sustaining,
rescuing love of God.

Blessing of Certain Hope
Isaiah 46:5-11; Romans 4:19-20

God, through Isaiah, addressed Israel's concerns about the conqueror, Cyrus. They would return home without full freedom or sovereignty. It was hard for Israel to accept a form of deliverance that did not solve the problem of national independence and a Davidic restoration. But Isaiah called Israel to a real faith: a faith that looks dismal facts in the face and still trusts God. Isaiah appealed to them to remember the Lord's record of bearing them on His shoulders and caring for them. They knew Him, even though they did not understand what He was doing.

In the name of Jesus Christ,
    I bless you with hope:
    the certainty and belief
    in One who carries you
    and cares for you.

I bless you with hope against all odds.
When you look facts in the face,
    even when there is bad news—
    frustration, disappointment, and sorrow—
    may you put your hope in God,
    and take Him at His word.
He will fulfill His promises.

Listen to what He says:

> *Who can you compare me to?*
> *Who is on the same level —*
> *has the same status and capacity?*
> *Who is even remotely similar to me*
> *or has anything in common with me?*

Stand firm and remember my past provision;
take it to heart, and fix it in your mind.
I am still the same as when I cared for you then.

I am God. I am the only God there is.
I am God. There is no other.
I declare the end from the beginning,
I dictate what will happen before it happens.

My purpose will be established,
and my plan is fixed.
Indeed, I have spoken.
Certainly, I will bring it to pass.
For sure, I will do what I have planned.

Anything you have put your hope in
    other than God will fail you;
    you will end up giving homage
    to something planned and created,
    even something made by human hands
    that must be picked up,
    carried, and set down.
Such a thing cannot answer your cries
    for intervention and help.

In light of the past,
    I bless you with understanding
    of the present and the future.
Recognize God's continuous actions:
    His love throughout history,
    His care and protection,
    His absolute commitment to you—
    making it unthinkable to believe
    that He will leave you now.

He is transcendent in glory and power:
    He is the fullness of the divine attributes,
    He is incomparable and irreplaceable,
    He is unique—none is like Him.
He is the God who is God.

You know Him, so obey Him.
Remember your history with Him:
    He delivered you, saved you
    and carried you in the past.
He will do the same in the present
    and into the future.

Blessing of a Heritage of Peace
Isaiah 54:11-13

In the name of Jesus Christ,
    I bless your spirit with peace—
    given and secured by Him.

When you were afflicted,
    He made you beautiful.
When you were lashed and buffeted
    by life's circumstances and hostilities,
    He made you secure on His foundation.
Today, you stand before Him
    dressed as royalty.

You now have peace with God
    and peace from earthly danger.
You have been set apart
    because you possess the word of God.

You have been given a heritage
    of priceless worth;
    all of your children will be taught
    by God Himself, and their peace
    will be secured in Him.

I declare a blessing on your children—
    children both natural and spiritual:
    they will have God to teach them,
    they will know divine well-being,
    they will live in great peace
    because their foundation is built on God.

Blessing of Joyful Transformation
Isaiah 55:6-13

In the name of Jesus Christ,
    I bless your spirit
    with the joy of being transformed
    in your heart and mind
    to align with God's word.

His thoughts are far higher than yours—
    they are beyond comparison,
    like the towering height of Heaven
    above the earth.
Yet you have been given
    access to what was once
    incomprehensible!

    Listen to Him:

    My word gives life.
    My word never fails —
    it accomplishes the purpose
    for which I sent it;
    it accomplishes what I desire,
    it completes the assignment I gave it.

When God speaks, He has given His word:
    His word cannot return empty.
His word accomplishes every purpose
    and completes every assignment He gave it.

I bless you with tenacity—
    seek to know the Lord,
    seek to know His thoughts and ways,
    speak His word of truth,

declare His word of certainty—of hope,
prophesy His word concerning the future,
and command His word into adversity.

Listen to the word of the Lord:

Go out with joy!
Be led with peace into a whole
and complete life—a new life.

As you are led by God, as you deepen
your relationship with Him,
you are transformed.
As you transform, creation transforms;
curses and death must bow to life.
Your culture will see your joy
and know you have been led with peace.

I bless you with renewing, transforming joy;
go out with joy,
be led by Peace.
I bless you with a whole and complete life.

Blessing of Transcendence
Isaiah 57:15

A humble (contrite) heart is a heart that has been crushed by life's burdens. This is the same kind of crushing the Messiah experienced in His suffering. Here, it refers to the suffering of those belonging to God.

I bless your spirit,
>in the name of Jesus Christ,
>with knowing the reality
>that He has come to dwell with you.
Because you have made God your refuge:
>you will know the enjoyment
>of His company, His security
>and His provision—
>you will inherit His promises.

I bless you with certainty
>when your present circumstance
>does not reflect your future hope.
Where life has crushed and humbled you,
>battered and bruised you,
>where suffering has brought you low,
>hear the word of the Lord:

>*I dwell in a high place, above all.*
>*And I also dwell with those who are crushed*
>*by life's burdens.*
>*I revive you—I give life to you.*

The exalted, eternal, holy God—
>transcendent and everlasting—
>dwells in you.
He has designed remedies

for the inequalities and injustice
you have faced.

I bless your spirit with the breath
of God, empowering you,
infusing your tenuous human life
with His eternal life.

Blessing of a Feast
Isaiah 58:13-14; Mark 2:27-28; Matthew 11:28

The meaning of Sabbath is "to rest." Isaiah relays God's definition of the Sabbath as an entire day designed for Him—a feast day. It was not to be a burden, weighed down by regulations. Sabbath was to be a time of "exquisite delight" in the Lord—a time set apart with joy to be captivated by Him.

Under the New Covenant, Jesus is our Sabbath Rest every day. As I read these Scriptures, I heard an invitation in my spirit from Holy Spirit: "Wake up in the morning and declare: Today is not a burden." I am practicing to have this mindset each morning ever since: "Today is not a burden. Today is a day of rest. Today is a day of delight. Today, I want to learn what it means to experience exquisite delight in you, Lord."

In the name of Jesus Christ,
    I bless your spirit with rest.
He is *Lord of the Sabbath;*
    He is your *Sabbath Rest.*

Set apart each day for God:
    a day of intimacy for Him and you—
    a feast day designed for joy
    with Him and family:
    a day of rest,
    a day of wholehearted devotion to Him,
    a day to learn what it means to have
    exquisite delight in Him.

I bless your spirit, soul, and body with rest.
Refuse to live like it is business as usual:
    running around here and there,

living to make money,
seeking your own pleasure,
speaking your own word,
wanting your own way.

Honor God by honoring one another
and by treating each day
as honorable and holy.
Live carefully and thoughtfully,
following divine direction—
devoting each day to Him.

Train for rest each day—a day
not designed to be a burden,
not to be weighed down by regulations.
Rest to work; work out of rest.

I bless you with confidence in Jesus
in the face of life.
Keep company with Him,
get away with Him,
walk with Him,
work with Him.
Watch how He works,
and you will recover your life;
you will learn to live freely
and lightly in His grace.

God has spoken—listen to His words:

Then I will cause you to soar above it all.
You will ride on the high hills of the earth.
I will feed you a feast from your inheritance:
you will walk in your covenant blessings,
you will enjoy and be satisfied
with the fulfillment of ancestral promises.

You are blessed with covenant blessings:
    discover them and walk in them.
I bless you with fulfillment
    of your ancestral promises.
I bless you with satisfaction
    in this feast day of intimacy with Jesus—
    a day of exquisite delight in Him.

Blessing of a Suddenly I
Isaiah 66:5-9; 2 Peter 3:3

God speaks of a supernatural birth without labor. He applies the principle of a painless birth to a supernatural birthing of a land and nation in a single day. In one day— or in a moment—means suddenly or instantaneously. He is rewarding and blessing those "who tremble at His word" and have a reverence for His word.

I recently had a vivid, prophetic dream. My husband, Garris and I were together as I delivered a baby. I experienced no pain, only excitement. I was struck with how carefree and joyful I felt, both for this birth and that there was no pain. I particularly felt joy knowing that this baby had been born right on time. I woke up feeling such gratitude that the birth was not premature but right on time. I knew it was a word for the Church. He was birthing a supernatural "suddenly" by His Spirit.

In the name of Jesus Christ,
    I bless you with participating
    in the plans devised by God
    and the sudden birthing of those plans—
    for you, your family,
    your city, and your nation.

Rather than voicing human wisdom
    with no foundation in the Word,
    I bless you with a profound love
    for God's word: His word is infallible.
He has pledged Himself
    to confirm and fulfill His word.
His word is the key to everything.

When skeptics mock His words,

resist their influence.
When it seems unrealistic
    to live by faith, contend to remain
    undistracted and undeterred.
When the waiting stretches on
    and there is no sign of breakthrough,
    hear God's word:

Before you go into labor,
before you experience pain—
you will give birth!
Have you heard of such a thing?
Have you seen such a miracle—
a land born in a moment,
a nation born in a day?
Will I bring my promise to the point of birth
and not let it be born?
You know me better than that.

I bless you with an upgrade of faith!

Blessing of a Suddenly II
Isaiah 66:5-9; 2 Peter 3:3

In the name of Jesus Christ,
    I bless you with expectancy
    and joyful certainty in your heart
    that what God said
    is going to come to pass.
He will act on your behalf.

Listen to His word:

    Will I bring my promise
    to the point of birth
    and then restrain it
    and not cause it to be born?

Does God purpose something only to abandon it?
Does He begin something and then frustrate it
    before it can move toward fulfillment?
Does He take a process almost to the end
    and not bring it to completion?

God is sovereign and He is your God:
    He is your divine certainty—
    He does not lie,
    He is the great *I AM*—
    the divine *I* who is in charge.
What can fail in Him? Nothing.

He does not change His mind about you
    or about His promises.
Make your decisions with that knowledge—
    order your affairs in anticipation
    of fulfillment of His word.

I bless you with sudden breakthrough:
 a supernaturally painless birth,
 a quickly born promise,
 an instant springing into being.

I bless you with healing;
 a spontaneous miracle in a moment,
 a family restored in an hour,
 a city saved in a day.

PART IV:
BLESSINGS FROM JEREMIAH & HAGGAI

Blessing of God's Original Plan
Jeremiah 29:1-14

When the Babylonians took captive the Israelites, God gave Israel a promise of deliverance through the prophet Jeremiah.

I bless your spirit,
    in the name of Jesus Christ,
    with God's original purposes
    and plans for your life.

I bless you with the help you need:
    with leaders stirred by His Spirit,
    with prophets of encouragement,
    with teachers of truth.

God is sovereign: He transcends
    your shortcomings,
    He plans for you deliverance,
    He prophesies your future.

Hear His words:

I will be there for you.
I will take care of you —
just as I promised.
I will deliver you right on time.

I will not abandon you;
I will bring you back home.
I have it all planned out —
plans for a sure, certain future,
a future you hoped for.

Call on me—come to me
and I will listen to you.
Seek me earnestly, diligently.
Search intensely with all your heart;
follow me closely.

I will make myself known to you.
I will turn things around—
I will restore your fortunes,
I will bring you back home.

Thrive and prosper as you wait in hope;
      plant gardens and eat their fruit,
      build houses and dwell in them,
      marry and have children—
      don't diminish—increase.
Seek peace wherever you are,
      even though it is not your true home;
      pray for its well-being,
      and things will also go well with you.

God's thoughts for you are for peace.
I bless you with the promise
      of a future and a hope—
      a certain future.

I bless you with a longing for God:
      seek Him with all your heart—
      pursue Him closely,
      as surely as He has pursued you.
You will not be disappointed—
      He will fulfill His promise
      right at the appointed time.

Blessings from Haggai

When the Israelites had been captive in Babylon for almost seventy years, God fulfilled His promise to set His people free. He moved the heart of King Cyrus of Babylon to issue an edict stating that Jews were free to return to Jerusalem to rebuild the Temple and the city. A faithful remnant responded, led by Zerubbabel.

The Book of Haggai records the rebuilding of the Temple. The returned exiles laid the foundation of the Temple but stopped after the second year; they were too overwhelmed by the opposition to their work and grew discouraged. Approximately 12 years later, God raised up prophetic ministers (Haggai and Zechariah) to help complete the reconstruction. It took 23 years from start to finish.

History records that God moved on three Kings to carry out His promise. The edict to rebuild the Temple and the city of Jerusalem was backed up with a wealth of gold and silver, supplies, support, and the return of what had been originally stolen from the Temple by Nebuchadnezzar.

Blessing of Response
Haggai 1:1-14

God has called each of us to specific responsibilities. These divine assignments can come under attack, and we will have to deal with difficulties, enemies, our selfish pursuits, and our own ways of making life work without God.

A few years ago, God changed the meaning of "responsibility" for me. I knew there is no freedom without responsibility, but I had experienced little freedom while trying so hard to be "responsible." My efforts were formed out of self-determinations and vows to improve and meet "the standard."

God said to me, "Instead of being responsible, be responsive to me. Respond to me, and you will be acting responsibly."

In the name of Jesus Christ,
 I bless your spirit with listening,
 your ears with hearing,
 and your heart with tuning in
 to the voice of God.

Hear God's word to you:

> *Think it over: did your growing disinterest*
> *in what I commissioned you to do*
> *turn you to your own ambitions?*

> *You have spent a lot of money*
> *without much to show for it.*
> *You fill your plate, but you are never full.*
> *You keep drinking, but you are still thirsty.*
> *You earn wages to put in a purse with holes,*

94

and nothing has come of it—
you are still dissatisfied.
You have been caught up
with taking care of yourself,
and you cannot thrive.

If what you were doing failed to flourish,
if anything was contaminated
because of a half-hearted response to me,
carefully consider putting me first
from this day forward.

May you respond to God's invitation.
If you started out strong and hopeful
    but were questioned, mocked,
      or even opposed for your efforts,
    are you discouraged?
If you are looking back in regret,
    comparing the past to the present,
    counting losses and unfulfilled hopes,
    are you disappointed in God?
If you got bogged down by the complexities
    of juggling life's assignments
    and responsibilities—have you lost interest
    in God's commission?

I bless you with courage;
    no longer be led by unbelief
    or a fear of lack.
Be responsive to God's Spirit;
    yield your being—all of who you are
    and all that you have
    to Him and to His Kingdom.

I encourage you to be strong—
    don't give up.

From this day forward,
    whatever you build,
    build with God.

Listen and hear His word:

> *I will show you what to do.*
> *Respond to me—I am with you!*

Blessing of Glory
Haggai 2:1-8; II Corinthians 3:16-18; Hebrews 12:25-28

The rebuilt Temple in Jerusalem did not begin to compare to Solomon's glorious Temple that had been destroyed. Many people wept with disappointment and discouragement. But the presence of the coming Messiah would cause the memory of Solomon's Temple to fade. The glory of Jesus' presence would remain, bringing great peace. We are living temples filled with His presence.

In the name of Jesus Christ,
    I bless your spirit
    with the glorious presence of the Lord
    made visible for all to see.

Listen to His Word:

> *I am with you — take courage.*
> *I am living and breathing,*
> *right here with you.*
> *Don't be afraid.*
> *Don't hold back.*

> *Be strong — I am with you.*
> *As I covenanted with you,*
> *I've given you authority*
> *and chosen you for this work.*

> *I am turning things upside down*
> *and starting over.*
> *I will release the wealth of the world*
> *to carry out what I have commissioned.*

I will fill this house with my glory.
You will be better at the end than when you began;
the end will be far more glorious than the beginning.
You will have a place of peace and wholeness,
and the glory of my presence.

God fills you with glory, and by that glory—
    which surpasses any previous glory—
    He transforms you into His image.
I bless you with this ministry
    of the New Covenant—
    the transcendent glory of Jesus Christ.

Because you have received mercy,
    be courageous, be completely honest,
    be willing to clear the blockages
    to the pathways of His love.
Only He can hold your heart
    without bruise or wound—
    only He can heal.

God has chosen you—His Spirit is upon you,
    He is with you—giving you authority
    and releasing provision.
Even as He shakes the systems of the world,
    honor Him: stand solidly and securely,
    receive your heritage—
    your rights to His unshakeable Kingdom.

BLESSINGS FROM THE NEW TESTAMENT

Gratitude is essential to joy. In fact, without being grateful, we cannot experience deep joy. I have only scratched the surface of gratitude and joy. I've discovered that gratitude is often an act of faith: setting my sights on the higher reality of God's invisible realm.

My circumstance may not be good, and I am not glad for trouble. Life doesn't owe me anything, but God is good (He is not the author of trouble); He is good all the time, and I can trust Him. All the good things in my life are gifts from Him, and if I am to continue to be thankful, I can't take them for granted. But if these truths about God are not settled in my heart, gratitude—the precursor to joy—is hard to come by.

Your mind is powerful. Neuroscientists have discovered what God has already said; the brain takes the shape of your thoughts. If your mind fills with worry, sadness, irritability, it will begin to take the shape of anxiety, depression, and anger. Everything you think creates connections within your brain. The more you repeat something, the stronger those connections grow. What flows through your mind is molding your brain, altering it in lasting ways.

Tell your brain to give thanks, and it will begin to take the shape of gratitude. Gratitude produces positive emotions like contentment, hope, and joy. Your emotions produce direct physical benefits through your immune and endocrine systems. Research confirms that gratitude affects every major organ system with potent health benefits.

Gratitude results in joy and generosity. We are destined to live under the blessings of God. We are being trained to receive His blessings and generously give out what has been given to us. We want to bless those we love—and bless those who don't deserve it or those who are our enemies.

The generosity of God is stunning. I can tell how difficult it is to accept and experience God's generosity by how small or large my capacity is to be generous. I cannot give out what I have not received.

Most of us are poor at receiving. Wherever we have fear, distrust, inability to love—in those places, we haven't received God's love. To the degree we receive, we have the capacity to give generously. Though it seems like the more we keep for ourselves, the happier we would be, we actually derive greater joy from giving generously, even sacrificially.

"The Great Reversal" refers to God's way of doing things—which is often the opposite of the way we would do them. Everything about grace and mercy seems upside down and backward to the natural mind, but our ways are not God's ways. His thoughts are higher than our thoughts.

We are learning Heaven's culture; we are given what we do not have, cannot work for, and do not deserve. Freely we have received—freely we are to give.

PART V:
BLESSINGS FROM MATTHEW

Blessing of Agreement
Matthew 5:43-47

In the name of Jesus Christ,
    I bless your spirit with choices
    that agree with His ways
    and His thoughts.

Respond in the opposite spirit
    to arguments, divisions, and complaints;
    to anger, frustration, and revenge.
Accept your mission to pray for those
    who come against you,
    mistreat and harass you.

Bless those you don't agree with,
    bless those who curse you,
    bless and love your enemies—
    do something wonderful for them
    in return for their hatred.

To join the chorus of complaints and anger
    joins you in agreement
    with the voice of the accuser,
    with the spirit of darkness,
    with the plans of the enemy.

May you choose words of life.
I bless you with abundance and wholeness—
    fully mature, lacking nothing,
    well-rounded, all-inclusive—
    as you use your voice
    for the things that matter the most to God.

May you focus your efforts on His agenda

and invite Holy Spirit
to examine your heart.
God is kind to all—
to those who do good or evil.
Come into agreement with His love
for all who cross your path.

You are a child of a perfect Father in Heaven—
in Him you are complete.
He wants to pour out blessings on you
and through you,
He wants to touch the world.

Blessing of the Life of God
Matthew 19:21-26

This blessing is inspired by the conversation Jesus had with a "rich young ruler." The ruler (possibly just out of his teens) was looking for eternal life, but not in the sense of life lasting forever; he was asking how he could "live a life belonging to God."

When the young man asked, "What do I lack?" Jesus answered in language he could understand by telling him to keep the commandments, specifically citing the last five laws dealing with his duty to others. The love of money kept the young man from following Jesus.

This story also revealed how impossible it was to live perfectly by following the Law. Jesus was teaching that salvation could only come by grace and grace is given only to the humble.

In the name of Jesus Christ,
> I bless your spirit with a quickening
> to what you see and hear of Him.

The essence of God is His love;
> the life of God is founded on love—
> an attitude of love,
> and a sacrificial generosity to others.

Jesus sees that your heart has been stirred:
> He sees your earnestness,
> your longing for God.
He sees your desire to live a life
> that belongs to Him—
> a life that reflects Him,
> a life like His.

He sees your need—
     your emptiness,
     your search for satisfaction,
     for happiness and serenity of heart.

Jesus sees deep inside you,
     far deeper than you have ever seen;
     He sees your hidden lack,
     and He has a solution for you.

In seeing you, He loves you;
     in loving you, He shows you your heart:
     the things you need to see,
     the things you must give up—
     if you are to follow God wholeheartedly.

I bless you with an awakening—
     see the lack behind your independence,
     your unbelief, your self-love,
     your greed, your idolatry.

I bless you with the gift of sight
     through your personal relationships.
Your attitude and actions toward others,
     reveal the true condition of your heart.
I bless you with sight
     so that healing can begin.

The essence of living the life of God
     does not come by carefully keeping the rules,
     or by calculating what you must do.
Your own efforts are powerless.

Set your heart on following Him—
     forsaking all, yielding all.
Without forsaking, there is no following.

God gives grace only to the humble;
     they are the only ones who can receive it.
I bless you with this key to a Life of God:
     any strength you have
     is the result of His grace.

Blessing of True Wealth
Matthew 19:21-26; Matthew 6:19-24

In Jesus' time, wealth was believed to be a sign of God's favor, which inferred that those with less did not have as much favor. The Rabbis would never have asked the "rich young ruler" to give up all his wealth. In fact, it was unlawful to give away all of one's possessions. At the most, you could only give away a fifth of what you owned.

This explains the disciples' surprise when Jesus told the young man that if he wished to enter a life with God, then he had to sell his possessions and give them to the poor. Then he would have treasure in Heaven and he could follow Jesus.

The disciples wondered, "Then what rich man can be saved?" Jesus was showing that the young man's great wealth had become a hindrance; it had become his identity, his status, his right, his idol, and his independence from the One True God.

The young man took Jesus's request like a death sentence to his life, instead of a call to life and living. He returned to his fine home that day, very poor and very sorrowful. We don't know his future, but we do know Jesus loved him—and he could have later become a follower of Jesus.

This encounter was not about money or wealth but about the heart. Our hearts will either lead us to God or to some form of addiction/idolatry. It could be the love of money or power or any other way we try to make life work without God.

Over my many years of pastoring, I have seen that money has a particular stranglehold on people, and it is usually the last thing we will yield to God. How we steward money is a very visible evidence of whether God is Lord of our lives or we are.

In the name of Jesus Christ,
    I bless your spirit with insight—
    with great spiritual understanding
    of your need for God
    and for His true riches.

There are things money cannot buy,
    and there are things from which
    money cannot save.
You cannot buy your way out of sorrow
    or buy your way into happiness.

Riches become dangerous if unyielded
    to Kingdom endeavors;
    they become a hindrance
    to discovering eternal treasure.

Your heart will always pursue
    what you value;
    your thoughts will always
    be focused on your treasure.

If riches take first place in your life,
    the void in your heart will be filled
    with something other than God.
Jesus will challenge you and confront you
    for your very own sake.
May the eyes of your spirit
    invite revelation light.

I bless you with your greatest Treasure—
    may His grace and generosity
    be your story.

Blessing of Generous Reward
Matthew 19:27-30; 20:1-16

Following the interaction with the rich, young ruler, Peter spoke up, claiming to have given up everything to follow Jesus. He wanted to know what his reward would be; he totally missed the heart of the conversation.

Jesus responded by telling a parable of God's generosity, reminding His listeners that on earth, you cannot measure how Heaven measures. He also warned the disciples not to think they would receive a greater privilege because they were the first. Those coming after them were to be equally rewarded.

This was a warning to the Jews who knew they were God's chosen people and looked down on the Gentiles. Jesus didn't want this mindset to be carried into the Church.

In the name of Jesus Christ,
    I bless your spirit
    with these words of Jesus:

> *Anyone who sacrifices all because of me*
> *will get it all back a hundred times over.*
> *They will also have eternal life.*

When you hand over everything to Jesus,
    you will receive back far more
    than anything you could give up.
Your reward will be a hundredfold
      according to Heaven's standards—
    beyond any measure here on earth.

I bless you with Heaven's economy:
    when you get picked last,

when you cannot earn enough,
when it is too late—
when you cannot make up for lost time,
these are the words of Jesus:

Many of the first will be last;
many of the last will be first.

God orchestrates His Great Reversal;
	He takes great pleasure in bestowing grace—
	not to diminish those blessed first,
	but to bless those who are chosen last.

In the divine sense,
	it is not about early or late.
Everyone ranks the same with God.

I bless you with endurance
	to remain at your post,
	faithful in your waiting
	even when time is growing short,
	when hope is dimming,
	when real needs for provision
	and promise become acute.

Everything God gives is grace—
	a gift you cannot earn:
	you cannot deserve it,
	you cannot measure it,
	you can only experience it.
Many will not understand this grace;
	some will compare
	and complain about it.

Your calling is to seek God and follow Him:
	search for Him more than great treasures,

seek Him more than great conquest:
be conquered by Him,
surrender all to Him.

I bless you with discovery
of Kingdom treasures
and with exhibiting
God's extravagant generosity.

Blessing of the Passion
Mathew 26:36-46; Hebrews 12:1-3

In the name of Jesus Christ,
    be encircled in His Passion.
I speak to your spirit:
    receive His love.

When your heart shatters
    under the weight of injustice,
    the sorrow of rejection,
    the injury of betrayal,
    the burning pain of abuse,
    the horror of evil,
    hear a sound from Heaven!

When your heart shuts down
    and you are buried alive,
    and the coffin nailed shut—
    when you are left in utter darkness,
    alone, forsaken, forgotten,
    separated from goodness—
    hear the Judge's gavel.
Hear the thunderous strike of justice
    in the courtroom of Heaven.

God will not overlook evil;
    someone must pay
    and justice must be served—
    so He sent Jesus.

Is what Jesus did enough?
Was His sacrifice and passion sufficient for you?
May your response be a resounding,
    Yes! I receive such Love.

PART VI:
BLESSINGS FROM MARK, LUKE & JOHN

Blessing of Harvest
Mark 4:3-20

In this parable, Jesus was asking His disciples to keep their hearts soft, enriched with nutrients like faith and hope, gratitude and joy. Even when you don't feel like it, you can cultivate your heart to produce great harvest.

In the name of Jesus Christ,
 I bless your spirit
 with Kingdom harvest.
May you intentionally welcome
 a ground turned over, tilled—
 a ground softened
 and enriched with nutrients,
 a ground thirsty for rain.

Be blessed with a softened heart—
 no longer motivated by your old nature,
 now wholehearted.

If your heart's soil is ready
 for the seed of God's word,
 you will always bear good fruit.

I bless your heart with an overflowing
 cornucopia of harvest.

Blessing of the Gift of Faith
Mark 4:13-20

It is one thing to be grateful for something you receive, it is another to be grateful as an act of faith—grateful for the as yet unseen and "unreceived."

In the name of Jesus Christ,
    I bless your spirit
    with the gift of faith.
Be so deeply rooted in His Word
    that you can wait in hope,
    destroying any thought
    that does not align with God.

Don't be disqualified from receiving
    the fulfillment of His word.
I bless you with a heart
    guarded from everything opposed to God:
    distractions and worries,
    self-pity and cynicism,
    bitterness and unbelief.

The goal of the enemy is to steal your faith,
    destroy the fulfillment of your destiny,
    and the destiny of your family line.
This battle is over territory and promise
    and great blessings.

The condition of your heart is paramount.
Every skirmish and fight
    carries the risk of offense,
    and offense hinders promise.
Blessing and offense do not work together.

Train for war and overcome:
    identify the tactics of your adversary,
    expose the trap set against you,
    refuse to live in offense at delays,
    at hardship or injustice.
Receive forgiveness for your own delays
    and learn how to avoid them.
Grant forgiveness and blessings.

I bless you with a heart of enriched soil—
    ready to receive God's promises,
    ready to plant, water, cultivate.
Jesus will deliver on His promise;
    listen to His words describing
    the result of your faith:

You will receive a thirty-fold,
a sixty-fold, or even
a hundred-fold harvest.

Blessing of Understanding
Mark 4:21-24

In the name of Jesus Christ,
    I bless you with light to see God's Word
    and to understand what it illuminates.
If you bring a hearing ear, you will hear.

I bless you with recognizing your need
    to understand His Word
    and to respond right away.

God's Word is a light to the world
    and won't be hidden;
    what is hidden will come to light,
    and all secrets will be exposed.

If you have understanding,
    don't live a hidden life,
    don't hide the truth,
    don't close your heart off to truth,
    or you will lose what little
    you think you have.

I bless you with diligence to understand
    the meaning behind everything
    you see and hear.
According to the depth of your longing
    to understand, much more
    will be added to you:
    receive the light of truth,
    live in the light of truth,
    love the light of truth
    and the Light will glow in you.

Blessing of Kingdom Growth
Mark 4:26-32

It is true that God's word never returns void. Those who are hungry for truth will come to understand the secrets of His Kingdom. Remember that the tiniest seed can be growing, unseen. You don't necessarily know how it took root, and you don't know when it will sprout. Sow seeds of gratitude for your sanity, good health, and a life of joy. To be grateful means you are more equipped to deal with situations that trigger anxiety.

In the name of Jesus Christ,
    I bless you with this mystery:
    God's Kingdom is like a seed,
    even the tiniest of seeds.
Don't despise small beginnings!

Plant truth from the realm of God's Kingdom—
    even the tiniest word of truth.
Plant that seed in good soil,
    and it will spring up,
    it will grow to full stature,
    it will provide great shade,
    and become the biggest tree in the garden.

I bless you with certainty in God's word.
Proclaim His Kingdom here on earth;
    here in your heart, and in your family.
His word rooted deeply will sprout and grow.
It is growing on the earth and not diminishing:
    it is growing in you and not diminishing.

Life is in the seed, and it will bear fruit
    when planted in good soul.

Declare what is not yet seen;
    it is already a reality, already growing.
I declare unprecedented growth;
    the harvest time has come!

Blessing of a Mantle
Luke 1:11-17 & 7:26-27; Malachi 3:1 & 4:5-6

In my spirit, I heard God say, "I restore family mantles." I was reminded of the mantle placed on John the Baptist, who became the last of the Old Covenant prophets and ushered in the transition to the New Covenant. His mantle was a Holy-Spirit-anointed calling and gifting.

God planned to give John that mantle before the foundations of the earth. Malachi prophesied about that mantle some 400 years before John's conception. God revealed His plan to John's father, Zacharias, before John was conceived. When John was born, Zacharias blessed his son with the prophesied mantle.

Like John, every family line has seen injustice and the resulting damage, affecting each successive generation. Decades—or even centuries—can pass in a family with no visible sign of a move of God.

And yet God planned for each one before He formed the foundations of the earth. Your parents did not create you, God did. He used their DNA to make you. Otherwise you would not be you—you would not exist. Despite unbelief or harmful choices in your family, you have a heritage that reaches back for centuries.

In your heritage are treasures waiting to be found, incrementally, over the course of your life. You have a calling on your life, an anointed mantle to step into. There are surprises of the Spirit, gifts and talents, all to be passed from generation to generation—both through your specific family line and through your spiritual sons and daughters. Remember that Elijah passed his mantle to Elisha, who then received a double portion.

But there is more! Those who have faith in Jesus Christ are children of Abraham and heirs of the promised blessings through his lineage (Galatians 3:7-9). By a rebirth from above, you have a new lineage, a new bloodline, and a new heritage through Jesus Christ. All of His divine nature has been imparted to you. All that is contained in Heaven is your inheritance!

Will you step up for your family and be the one to receive your God-ordained mantle?

In the name of Jesus Christ,
    I bless you with the restoration
    of your family mantle.
Discover God's destiny for you—
    His purposes and plans,
    His callings and gifts
    ordained through your lineage.

I bless you with God's inner strength:
    His self-control and discipline
    to overcome any obstacles
    found in your generational line.

Don't resent your past,
    don't be held back by self-pity,
    don't give up,
    don't let unbelief silence your voice.

It may have been decades, even centuries,
    since your family line knew
    a move of God's Spirit,
    but He will have the last word.

If you let Him, He will use your sorrows
    as your most defining moments,
    as your greatest breakthroughs,
    as ground zero for His power and glory.

Embrace your family lineage;

stand in the gap
and forgive your forefathers,
ask forgiveness for your participation
in the same rebellion, unbelief,
or hardheartedness.

You no longer are disadvantaged;
you are not an orphan—
you are not all alone.
You are blessed with belonging
to God's family;
you are blessed with all
that is contained in Heaven.

Like John the Baptist,
you too are called to announce
Jesus to the world.
You are called to bring reconciliation to families.

Pass God's blessings on—
impart your grace and love,
impart your gifts and anointing,
impart your heritage—your mantle—
a double blessing to those who follow after you.

Blessing of Unity
Luke 1:17; Malachi 4:5-6

In the name of Jesus Christ,
    I bless your spirit with power,
    and the anointing of unity,
    like that of John the Baptist.
Be a forerunner for future generations.

May you be instrumental
    in turning the hearts of the fathers—
    with strength-in-tenderness—
    back to their children
    and the hearts of the disobedient
    back to the wisdom of their righteous fathers.

May you help to heal the hearts
    of fathers and mothers
    who are not tender and loving
    to their own children—
    having never known
    or received love themselves.

By the anointing of God's Spirit,
    be blessed with authority to persuade
    and prepare children, young and old,
    to turn back to the Lord their God,
    to reconcile with their fathers and mothers,
    to be a united people—
    ready for God's manifest presence.

Blessing of Promise
Luke 2:25-33

Simeon lived his life by promise, led by God's Spirit.

In the name of Jesus Christ,
    I bless your spirit
    with prayerful expectancy
    of God's promises.
He will not delay; live your life
    to the end of your days
    believing His word.

I bless you with a coming-upon-you
    of the Holy Spirit—
    empowering you, gifting you,
    showing you things to come.

May the prophetic expression of your words
    align with God's promise
    and be a light that shines on your steps,
    your pathway, your journey,
    until their appointed time.

I bless you with stories of fulfilled promises.
Be like Simeon, as one led by God's Spirit,
    announcing Jesus Christ to your culture.
Live a story that will be told and multiplied
    throughout all coming generations.

Blessing of Sacrifice
Luke 21:1-4

I heard the story of a missionary who served in a village stricken with debilitating poverty. Nothing seemed to release the church there from decades of lack. The missionary couldn't bring himself to teach on giving. After all, the people had so little—how could he ask for anything? Instead, he tried to meet needs whenever he could.

One day, Holy Spirit clearly instructed him to teach on giving as a way of life. The missionary was to teach generosity because Father God was generous. The missionary obeyed and taught on the heart of giving and investing in the Kingdom of God. The people had no money, but they began bringing chickens and vegetables from their gardens, which the missionary was able to distribute to the more destitute.

Everything shifted. The church community—and then the village—made an undeniable and dramatic turnaround as a result of their generosity. Generations of poverty no longer could hold them down. Blessings of favor increased in all dimensions.

In the name of Jesus Christ,
    I bless your spirit
    with sacrificial giving:
    giving all into His hands—
    all that you are and all that you have.
God will anoint and empower
    your stewardship.

When you put what you "own"
    into His care and keeping,
    He takes full responsibility

to multiply and bless His belongings;
in His hands, all is safeguarded.

He is free to use what you have given Him
to free you from fear,
to train you for generosity,
to touch those in need,
to influence the nations.

The return on investing in the Kingdom
cannot be measured by earthly standards;
it is a return on your generous giving
that cannot be explained
with financial savvy.
You cannot out-give God.

I bless you with sacrificial giving,
not just out of your earthly surplus.
You are not giving to please man,
you are not giving to be noticed,
you are not giving to earn your way.
Give—directed by the Holy Spirit.

I bless you with increase,
with debts paid off and no future debt,
with multiplication of resources
to pour more into the Kingdom of God—
to be a blessing,
to be even more generous.

I bless you with joy in giving.
May it be said of you what Jesus
said of the widow:
She has given more than all of them.
She gave sacrificially and it was recorded
for all the ages.

Blessing of Belief
John 12:44-50

In the last public teaching of Jesus, He shouted out passionately that believing in Him and the words He spoke meant believing in God.

In the name of Jesus Christ,
    I bless your spirit with belief in Him.
When you see Jesus,
        you are seeing the One who sent Him;
        you are looking into the face of God.

When you believe in Jesus,
        you are believing in God:
        you will no longer wander in darkness,
        you will no longer dwell in gloom,
        you will no longer live in obscurity,
        you will no longer
    be ignorant of divine truth.

Do you hear the heartbeat of the Father?
Without Jesus, you will dwell
        in total absence of light—
        without spiritual perception.
God does not want that for you.

If you ignore and reject the invitation
        to believe in Jesus the Messiah—
        He does not judge you.
Listen to His words:

    If you reject me,
    if you reject my words,
    if you don't take me seriously —

I don't reject you.
I did not come to judge you.
I came to save you.

True love requires your choice.
You will have to live or die
    with the decision you make:
    will you choose to accept Him
    or will you choose to reject Him
    and reject real and eternal life?

On the final day of Judgment,
    the message of truth Jesus has given you
    will rise up to judge your choice.
He will not make that decision for you—
    you will decide.

Jesus invites you to the light—
    to believe in Him,
    to entrust yourself to Him.
Darkness equals unhappiness—
    light equals happiness.

I bless you with belief in Jesus.
He is not just speaking words of life;
    He is the Eternal Word.
    He is the last Word.

May you choose Jesus the Messiah:
    choose light,
    choose happiness,
    choose eternity with Him.

PART VII:
BLESSINGS FROM II CORINTHIANS

Blessing of Exchange I
II Corinthians 4:6-18

How would you live your life if "the weight of the world" on your shoulders was exchanged for a weight of glory beyond all measure?

In the name of Jesus Christ,
> I bless your spirit with Heaven's vantage—
> focus your attention on what is unseen.

God said, *Let brilliant light shine out of darkness.*
Now He lights up your life—
> His cascading light flows into you
> as you gaze into the face of Jesus.

I bless you with this new perspective—
> exchange the weight of your distress
> for the weight of glory.
Use your distress to prepare yourself
> to experience His glory.

See your problem like a trainer
> who is by your side—
> drawing you into the invisible realm,
> giving you glimpses
> of heavenly places with Jesus.

I bless you with seeing
> all that God is accomplishing
> through this difficulty;
> seeing that any and every kind of pressure
> does not crush you.

You may not know what to do,

but God knows what to do—
so don't quit:
you may be knocked down, but not out,
you may be corrected, but not condemned.
Your struggle will lose its power
to drag you down.

Even if you are spiritually terrorized—
you know God has not left your side.
His life is all the more evident in you;
every detail works to your advantage.

Be overwhelmingly blessed
with the life of Jesus in you;
a Treasure seen daily in you—
accompanied with such an extraordinary,
overflow of power,
it is seen as His, not yours.

I bless your inner being with daily renewal;
not a day goes by
without God's unfolding grace.
I bless you in your preparation
for a glory that cannot be calculated—
so massive there are no comparisons,
so vast and transcendent
that blessedness never ends!

Blessing of Exchange II
II Corinthians 5:17-21; Romans 6:22-23

In the name of Jesus Christ,
    I bless your spirit
    with God's eternal exchange;
    exchange all aspects of your fallen nature
    for His divine nature.
Jesus carried you and your sin to the grave,
    and you rose to new life with Him.

Experience His exchange:
    fear for His love,
    hopelessness for His certain future,
    worthlessness for His worth,
    rejection for His acceptance,
    grief for His comfort,
    helplessness for His power,
    shame for His dignity and significance,
    separation for His reconciliation,
    taintedness for His innocence,
    voicelessness for His words of authority,
    sickness for His health,
    insufficiency for His abundance,
    victimization for His overcoming grace,
    curses for His blessing.

I bless you with courage to truly live
    in the full light of mercy:
    be loved and love,
    be forgiven and forgive,
    be comforted and comfort,
    be renewed to the new you.

Blessing of Spiritual Weapons
II Corinthians 10:3-6

*This blessing is for the spiritual battles throughout family
generations, but it covers all aspects of life.*

In the name of Jesus Christ,
    I bless your spirit
    with spiritual weapons of warfare
    to wage a campaign of liberty
    for your family.

You have been placed in your family
    for such a time as this;
    you are not an accident.

You live in the natural realm,
    but you don't use human weapons;
    you don't use manipulation
    to achieve your aims.
You have spiritual weapons,
    energized with divine power
    to dismantle defenses and strongholds
    built up over the generations.

Armed with such dynamic weaponry,
    you can expose and abolish
    any rebellion perpetrated in your lineage—
    anything kept hidden in the dark.

I bless you with strategies to demolish
    every deceptive fantasy opposing God.
Break down every attitude that defies
    the true knowledge of God.
Take captive every thought—

insist that it bow in obedience
to the Anointed One.
None will have power over you.

I bless you with redemptive eyes
to see your family strengths,
characteristics, talents, gifting,
ethnicity, and nationality—
reframing them into blessings.

I bless you with the fruit
of intercessory prayers
in your ancestral line
going back through the centuries.

God prepared this place
and time for you in advance—
to love you,
to be one with you,
to partner with you
and save your family.

Blessing in Listening Prayer
II Corinthians 10:5; I John 1:7; John 6:44-45

When I ask God for wisdom, I often command any demonic interference to be silenced—to have no part in the conversation. It is helpful to identify demonic input, my own mindset, or the voices of others when addressing false beliefs that may inform my thinking and actions. But when I want to hear only the voice of God, I will pray the prayer couched in this blessing.

Some years ago, I was in conversation with a pastor about the inner healing ministry I call Listening Prayer, that I have been part of since 2001. The pastor handed me a little book called God Guides *by Mary Geehe, a missionary to India from 1924 to 1962.*

When arriving in India for the first time, Miss Geehe faced many cultural and religious barriers. She was completely overwhelmed with an impossible task. To make it worse, the long-time, local missionary was leaving for a year of furlough, and she was somehow supposed to cover for him. His parting advice was to listen to God. Having nowhere else to turn, she learned to listen to God for everything. Her experiences tell of God's faithfulness, humor, tenderness, and power.

Her instructions were to have pen and paper in hand when listening to God. What do you want to ask God? Be Specific. Take the time to listen. Write down what you sense God is saying. If you have a prayer partner, compare notes when you are each done listening. If you receive any directives, obey God, and God will act on your behalf.

In the name of Jesus Christ,
    I bless your spirit
    with being taught directly from Him:
    He is pure light, He is pure truth,

He is pure love—
He will put you together
and set you on your feet.

If anyone has anything against you,
    first be reconciled.
If you hold any offense, forgive;
    the offender and the one offended
    must each face their own motives and actions.

I bless you with ears to hear God's voice:
    draw close to Him and listen attentively.
Take the quickest route
    to be present with Him.

Quiet all other voices, speaking this:

In the name of Jesus Christ,
who has all authority and power,
I speak to any demonic spirits
aligned against me/us:
I command you to step aside;
be silent, deaf, blind—
cut off in every sense
from this conversation.

Jesus, I renounce any thinking of my own
that opposes you and your truth.
I command my thoughts—
my way of thinking,
my ideas and imaginations—
to submit to your Lordship.

I ask you for wisdom:
I am listening for your direction—
identify what you want me to see,

and reveal your truth to me.

I bless you with being taught and led
 in all things by the Holy Spirit;
 you are blessed as you wait
 for guidance into all truth.

I bless you with courage born of love
 to respond to the voice of God;
 agree with His directives,
 take each step in the right order,
 and obey quickly.

Ask and then listen to God;
 when God speaks, obey.
Here is a reality;
 when you obey, God acts;
 when God acts, everything changes.

Blessing of Grace Power
II Corinthians 11:23-33

In the name of Jesus Christ,
    I bless your spirit with His grace—
    His grace becomes more apparent
    in your weakness.

In order to receive grace,
    recognize your need for grace.
Jesus has front-loaded you with grace;
    see Him right there with you
    in the middle of the struggle.
Experience His ability to strengthen you.
Experience more breakthrough.

I bless you with grace power
    when you deal with harassment or attack,
    when constantly misunderstood,
    when enduring hindrances,
    when experiencing great difficulties
    and dangerous situations.

I bless you with grace power
    in all situational opposition:
    when you are at your most vulnerable,
    when worked to the point of exhaustion,
    when you face many sleepless nights,
    when left hungry and exposed to the cold.

I bless you with grace power
    when you are overwhelmed with sorrow,
    when you deal with the daily pressures,
    when you are weighed down with concern
    for the welfare of others.

In receiving and relying on grace,
    grace flows through you.
God's grace is power—
    a power released in your powerlessness,
    a joy interjected into your joylessness,
    a hope dispelling your hopelessness,
    a gift of faith disarming unbelief.

Blessing of Celebration
II Corinthians 12:7-10

I never could relate to this Scripture until I began to worship God right in the middle of my struggles, using each and every struggle as the catalyst to run to Jesus and get face to face with Him. My first and primary goal was to see Him and His love for me. I was always touched in some way, with a resulting quiet and peace.

Some years had gone by, when one day, feeling vulnerable and sad because of failing again, I did what I had been practicing—I thanked Jesus for identifying any feeling that was an obstacle to His love. I thanked Him for conviction (sight) that produced godly sorrow. I thanked Him for His undeniable goodness, His mercy, His kindness.

While absorbed in the beauty of His comfort and celebrating His mercy, glad that I was no longer blinded by condemnation, I experienced something for the first time in the middle of difficulty: joy. Joy came bubbling up out of my spirit. Joy is knowing that you are truly, unconditionally loved.

It has been my observation that our biggest obstacle is not the enemy or our weaknesses. It is the refusal to accept God's love and grace right in the middle of the fray.

In the name of Jesus Christ,
    I bless your spirit, soul, and body
    with the shelter of His power
    resting upon you.
Your weakness becomes a portal
    to God's power.

Listen to His words:

My grace is sufficient for you —
it is more than enough.
My power is fully expressed
in your weakness.

You are not defeated by your weakness;
    instead, you will sense more deeply
    the mighty power
    of Jesus Christ living in you.

Celebrate Him in the middle of your struggle.
I bless you with joy in Him, even when
    you are surrounded by troubles.

Your reception of His love for you
    has made you even stronger—
    His strength plus your weakness
    equals strength.

PART VIII:
BLESSINGS FROM EPHESIANS, PHILIPPIANS & I TIMOTHY

Blessings from Ephesians

I entered eighth grade in 1963. My family had come to Seattle, Washington for a year-long furlough from missions in Central America. I went from a culture where no one I knew spoke English to a culture where no one I knew spoke Spanish. I had only one or two memories of the US from when I was three years old, and I had vivid memories from when we had come "home" on furlough for my first-grade school year.

Now I was twelve and experiencing many "firsts." I talked on the telephone for the first time. I watched color TV for the first time—especially enjoying Superman *and* Sea Hunt. *And for the first time, I started listening to the music of the era, like the Beatles. I particularly enjoyed listening to my radio before bedtime.*

One of Doris Day's songs caught my imagination, and I sung along to the lyrics: "Que sera, sera—whatever will be, will be. The future's not ours to see. Que sera, sera—whatever will be, will be." I think part of the song's attraction for me was the Spanish lyrics. I hummed and sang that little ditty a lot. One day my Dad interrupted me and told me not to sing it anymore. I was surprised and a little hurt. I don't remember an explanation—just that he did not approve. He didn't often correct me, which made this reprimand stick with me.

Many years later, I understood why Dad disliked the words of that chorus. He was right. When I sang it, I was prophesying a nicely packaged lie, even though I knew nothing about prophecy. God tells me His plans for my destiny. Before the foundation of the world, I was planned for—for such a time as this. I was no accident left to the whims of wistful thinking. There was no "que sera, sera" about my life.

These blessings from Ephesians are about the destiny we have in God.

Blessing of Devotion
Ephesians 1:1-6

Every human is created in the image of God. Before the foundation of the world, you were spoken into being; you were chosen by a word to be a word. When God created you, He had already chosen you. He waits for you to respond to His gift of deliverance, salvation, and healing.

In the name of Jesus Christ,
>   I bless your spirit with devotion to God—
>   He has always had you in mind:
>   He is devoted to you,
>   He made you one with Jesus—
>   the Anointed One,
>   He made you whole and holy.

I bless you with God's release of grace—
>   His extravagant, cascading grace
>   that imparts peace, tranquility,
>   and total well-being.
Everything Heaven contains
>   has already been poured out upon you.

From the very beginning—
>   before the foundation of the universe—
>   God spoke you into being,
>   He joined you to Himself,
>   and He chose you to be His very own.

From the very beginning,
>   you were destined to be created;
>   God marked you with His love
>   and set you apart.

In His great love for you—
　　God ordained you to be one with Jesus;
　　He delighted in adopting you
　　and establishing you as His child
　　through your oneness with Jesus.

You have always been the focus of His love.
Now, no longer separated from each other,
　　you are seen as holy in His eyes,
　　with unstained innocence.

The Father's love for His Beloved Son
　　is the same love He has for you;
　　His devotion for His Son
　　is the same as His devotion for you.
I bless you with receiving such love!

Blessing of Wellbeing
Ephesians 1:5-10

You are joined to Jesus Christ
    because of His sacrifice—
    His blood poured out
    on the altar of the Cross.

In His name, I bless your spirit
    with the treasures of His super-grace,
    already working powerfully in you:
    you are free,
    you are completely free,
    you are abundantly free
    of all penalties and punishment!

God thought of everything for you;
    He provided everything
    you could possibly need.
He told you His hidden mysteries—
    letting you in on His plans
    from the beginning of time.

He told you His secret, delightful desires—
    to flood you with His love,
    to infuse His grace
    into every part of your being,
    to release to you all forms of wisdom
    and practical understanding.

I bless you with a deep sense of wellbeing,
    knowing that God's detailed plan
    will reign supreme through every season,
    until He makes all things new
    in all of Heaven and earth through Jesus Christ.

Blessing of Destiny
Ephesians 1:11-14

All that Jesus Christ does
    honors His Father.
It is in His name that I bless you
    with the fullness of your destiny—
    in Him you find out who you are
    and what you are living for.

God ordained you
    to be His own inheritance
    through your union with Jesus.
He gave you your destiny
    before you were even born.
He had His eye on you
    before you even heard of Jesus.
He had glorious designs for your life—
    designs possible for you to fulfill.
He always accomplishes every purpose
    and every plan in His heart.

I bless you with hope in Jesus Christ—
    a certainty of hope.
Be certain about your inheritance;
    such hope is a promise,
    such promise is the Holy Spirit,
    and Holy Spirit is the guarantee
    of the rights of your covenant.

I bless you with the longing
    to live in your hope-promise—
    your inheritance:
    here on earth as it is in Heaven.

Blessing of God's Riches
Ephesians 1:17-22

In the name of Jesus Christ,
    I bless your spirit with the unveiling
    of His riches—His Spirit of wisdom,
    His Spirit of revelation.

In your deepening intimacy with Jesus,
    I bless you with His light
    illuminating the eyes of your imagination—
    flooding you with focused clarity.

See what He is calling you to do,
    grasp the immensity of His calling,
    live with certainty of His presence,
    experience the full revelation of your hope.

I bless you with moment-by-moment faith
    to experience His measureless, mighty,
    explosive resurrection power.
God raised Jesus Christ from the dead—
    giving Him supreme authority
    and the highest honor
    on earth and in all the heavenly realms.

God has put everything
    under the authority of His Son.
Jesus is sovereign over everything—forever:
    He runs the universe,
    from governments to galaxies,
    He has the final word on everything.

With His presence flowing through you—
    through His Church—

Jesus speaks and acts and fills all things.
I bless you with an intimate relationship
    with the Leader and Source
    of everything you need.

You are blessed by His presence
    flowing through you,
    His fullness filling you.
You are His true inheritance!

Blessing of Compassion
Ephesians 2:4-10

In the name of Jesus Christ,
    I bless your spirit
    with openness and reception
    to God's compassion and mercy.

In the past, you let the world—
    which doesn't know
    the first thing about living—
    tell you how to live.
We all did this: we did what we felt like doing,
    when we felt like doing it.

But even when you were dead
    and doomed in your many sins,
    God united you into the life of Jesus—
    joining you together as one.

God immersed you in His mercy,
    He embraced you
    with His incredible love.
He saved you—picking you up,
    raising you up, and setting you
    into the highest Heaven—
    in the company of Jesus.

You cannot earn this salvation—
    God gave you the authority
    to be there with Jesus;
    saving you is His idea,
    His work, and His gift.

Now that you are joined to Jesus,

I bless you with your new reality—
I bless you with a visible display
of God's infinite, limitless compassion
showered upon you.

I bless you with a life written by God—
an epic poem
crafted by the Word, Himself.

Blessing of Limitlessness
Ephesians 3:14-20

My life's focus is to understand and respond to this message and then to help others do the same.

In the name of Jesus Christ,
 I bless your spirit with an outpouring
 of God's limitless riches,
 His limitless glory,
 His limitless favor.

I bless you with His strength
 to open the door of your heart
 and invite Him in—
 until His supernatural strength,
 His divine might,
 and His explosive power
 flood your inner being.

You are the resting place of His love—
 His love is the secure
 and ever-expanding
 foundation of your life.
Be grounded and growing in love.

May you be able to take in
 the astonishing magnitude of His love:
 how intimate, how enduring,
 how far-reaching, how inclusive,
 how endless, how immeasurable it is—
 transcending your understanding!

I bless you with an outpouring
 of His extravagant love,

until you are filled to overflowing—
until you are filled with the fullness of God.

His miraculous might constantly empowers you:
    He will outdo your greatest request,
    He will exceed your most unbelievable dream,
    He will go infinitely above and beyond
    your wildest imagination.

Blessing of Mighty Power
Ephesians 3:20

In the name of Jesus Christ,
    I bless your spirit
    with God's mighty power;
    His ability to work in you
    and accomplish all that He says.

I bless you with vision to see His radical
    and outrageous displays of love,
    that are so much bigger,
    that are so much greater,
    that only He can do—
    more than you could begin to imagine.

He has plans to lift you higher:
    plans for oneness of heart and mind,
    plans for your future that are certain.

I speak to your disappointment,
    your weariness, your hurt,
    your hope deferred:

    Come Breath of God,
    breathe light into the darkness,
    breathe your supernatural strength,
    breathe your breath of life—of love.

I speak to your frustration,
    your anger,
    your rage at injustice:

    Come Breath of God,
    breathe your mercy and justice,

your redemption,
your full restoration.

I speak to your confusion,
    your disorientation,
    your misunderstandings:

   Come Breath of God,
   breathe wisdom and clarity,
   breathe your passion and joy.

I bless you with God-dreams and visions
    and seeing their fulfillment
    for your lifetime,
    and for future generations—
    because He is that faithful and good.

Blessing of Divine Invitation
Philippians 3:7-16

I've heard people use this Scripture as a reason to not deal with their past issues. However, Paul is talking about no longer boasting in his past accomplishments and the fact that he could trace his family line all the way back to Abraham. His identity was now based on experiencing oneness with Jesus.

Whatever is not reconciled in your past is still speaking to you and motivating you in the present. Invite Jesus' healing grace into your past. You and He dwell together outside of the restrictions of the dimension of time. Let Him address and inform your past, present, and future from His and your position in eternity.

In the name of Jesus Christ,
 I bless your spirit with continual longing
 to know Him more fully—
 more intimately.
Run with passion into His abundance.

Respond to His invitation—
 accept His offer
 to experience the power
 of His life working in you.

I bless you with experiencing oneness with Jesus:
 be one with Him in His sufferings,
 be one with Him in His death.
Know complete oneness with Him,
 rising from the realm of death.

No longer trust in your own power,
 strength, common sense, talents,

natural strengths, abilities,
personality, appearance, wit,
intelligence, education,
or status in society.

To truly know Jesus Christ in all His greatness
and to embrace Him as Lord
means letting go:
let go of all your past boasting,
all the accomplishments you took credit for,
all that you thought made you
better than others.
Regard it all as nothing in comparison
to real wonderment
that Jesus is your Lord.

I bless you with one compelling focus:
forget the past as you fasten your heart
to the future with Him.
Be consumed by Him,
rich in the reality of knowing Him,
embracing Him in all His greatness.

I bless you with advancement—
following one path with one passion.
Run straight to His divine invitation
to discover all He wants to reveal,
and to reach the purpose
He has called you to fulfill.

Blessing of Gratitude
Philippians 4:4-7

This life-Scripture in Philippians has helped produce more celebration for me in every season.

In the name of Jesus Christ,
    I bless your spirit
    with joyful celebration.
Celebrate God all day, every day.
In every season, be cheerful—
    let joy overflow because you
    are united with the Anointed One!

May you experience intimate closeness
    with Jesus who is always near you:
    walk with Him, talk with Him,
    listen to Him—
    be saturated in prayer
    and overflowing with gratitude.

I bless you with unity
    flowing into every relationship,
    as you work in unity—
    with and for each other—
    in gentleness, humility, and fairness.

Instead of worrying about everything,
    thank God He is right there,
    ready to partner with you.
Gratitude is a pathway of sight
    into the invisible realm.

As you focus your attention on God,
    He will make Himself known to you:

He will displace fear with love,
He will swap doubt with faith.
He will guard your heart
from within and without.
He will mend your heart
to wholeness.

I bless you with surrender:
yield your rights, your demands,
your determinations, and your will
to the Lord of lords
and the King of kings.
Jesus has already gone before you
and taken care of everything for you.

I bless your heart and mind
with moment-to-moment focus:
practice being aware of His presence,
fasten your thinking on Him,
thank Him for His goodness
and His mercy to give you sight
of what is standing in the way of Love.

He is your joy center—I bless you with deep joy:
He is your truest reality—
authentic and honorable,
noble and reputable,
compelling and gracious,
beautiful and awesome,
pure and holy, merciful and kind.

Gratitude is a precursor to peace,
peace will displace worry
at the core of your being.
I bless you with single-hearted vision
for Joy and Peace, Himself.

Blessing of Mercy's Kiss
I Timothy 1:1-2, 13-17

In the name of Jesus Christ,
    I bless your spirit
    with the kiss of God's mercy,
    His breath of love,
    His word of life.

He loves you despite your rebellion:
    even when you scorned
    what turned out to be true,
    even when you were ignorant
    and didn't know what you were doing.

Jesus continually loves you;
    He brought you back to life.
I bless you with full faith and love for Him,
    now that you are captured by grace.

May you live out His desire for you,
    displaying the outpouring
    of His Spirit through you,
    and fulfilling the Law of love.
Love deeply with a pure heart,
    with a clean conscience,
    with the truths of your faith.

Let your worship rise to the only God—
    to the invisible King of all the universe,
    the One who is indestructible,
    the One who is full of glory,
    the One who is worthy of the highest honor
    throughout all of time and eternity.

Jesus Christ is your living Hope—
    your Mercy-Giver.
I decree over your life today
    incredible grace,
    abundant mercy,
    and total well-being
    from Abba, Father
    and the Anointed One, Jesus.

Blessing of Prophecies
I Timothy 1:11,15 & 18-19; Psalm 119:104-105 & 130

Prophecies are promises in the process of fulfillment. We wage spiritual warfare by using these prophecies as weapons.

In the name of Jesus Christ,
> I bless your spirit
> with His words of prophesy.
God's words are true—lighting up
> your steps and pathway.

Recall His prophecies once given to you;
> they are in the process of fulfillment.
Hold on to those prophecies,
> declare them, use them as weapons
> so that you can wage spiritual battles.

I bless you with faith
> to partner with God's promises.
Proclaim His word over yourself
> and your family.
Proclaim His directives over your city,
> your nation, the world.

God's truth deserves to be received by all.
I bless you with a commissioning
> to preach and prophesy
> the wonderful news
> of God's glory and presence.
May you be continually empowered
> and authorized to be His partner in ministry.

PART IX:
BLESSINGS FROM HEBREWS

Blessing of God's Language
Hebrews 1:1-3

In the name of Jesus Christ,
    I bless your spirit with Heaven's language;
    the language God now uses to speak to you.
Jesus is the language of God:
    God now speaks to you openly
    in the language of His Son—
    He speaks through His Son.
Jesus is the mirror image of God:
    the exact expression of His true nature,
    the brilliant radiance of His splendor,
    the out-shining of His glory.

Jesus is seated on the highest throne
    at the right hand of God.
Through Him, God created the panorama
    of all time and all things.
By the power of His words,
    He created and coordinated
    the universe, beautifully:
    He crafted the cosmos,
    He framed the worlds—
    prepared and arranged them.
He holds everything together
    and expands it all by His powerful words.

Jesus—the Messiah, the Living Word,
    the Creator—made you His family
    and gave you His language.
May your words be His words,
    speaking in the Son's language,
    speaking His truth in love.

Blessing of Boldness
Hebrews 10:19-23; Song of Songs 4:9

In the name of Jesus Christ,
    I bless your spirit with boldness.
Through the blood of Jesus,
    you have a new, life-giving way:
    you have a free access
    to the heavenly realm,
    you are welcomed
    into the most holy sanctuary.
Your magnificent King-Priest
    welcomes you into His House.

May you be fully convinced
    that nothing will keep you
    at a distance from Him.
Your heart has been sprinkled
    with His blood,
    your impurity has been removed,
    and you have been freed
    from an accusing conscience.
You have been made innocent—
    clean and presentable to God,
    inside and out.

God always keeps His promises,
    so hold tightly to hope living in you.
I bless you with acts of faith—
    come without hesitation,
    come closer with an open heart,
    approach with great boldness;
    be a fearless lover of His heart.

Blessing of Faith
Hebrews 10:26-39; Habakkuk 2:3-4

The quote, "live by faith," is from the Book of Habakkuk. The author of Hebrews is telling the Church to live by faith and not be held back by fear. The word for fear here means a cowering fear that would compromise the people's faithfulness to God. We must live by faith—by loyal trust. If we cut and run, we lose out. It gives God no pleasure that we would miss out on His favor.

In the name of Jesus Christ,
    I bless your spirit
    with upgrades in your faith.
It is who you believe in
    and what you believe
    that makes the difference.

Your faith is destined for great reward;
    you possess great things in Heaven—
    you possess a growing treasure
    that can never be taken from you.

When you have known and received the truth,
    don't persist in deliberate sin.
Don't trample the Son of God
    under your feet, scorning the blood
    of the New Covenant that made you holy,
    mocking the Spirit who gives you grace.
There will be a day before the Living God
    when you will give account for your acts.

Remember when you first encountered
    the Light shining on your heart?
Remember your first touch from Love—

when you were overcome
by Extravagant Grace?
Remember your first love.

I bless you with a steady faith—
     a courageous, loyal trust in God.
Even if you are persecuted for your belief,
     accept those violations with joy.

Those attempting to find life in themselves
     are full of self but soul-empty:
     their soul is not right within them,
     their nature is transient and unstable,
     their fear will debilitate them.
Their life is like hell and death—their desire
     for more will never be satisfied.

But you are not cowering in fear—
     you are not perishing;
     you are among those
     who live by faith
     and who experience true life.

I bless you with strength of endurance
     to reveal the poetry of God's will;
     to express the nuances, the intricacies,
     the beauty, the simplicity, the directness,
     the depth, the wonder, and the intimacy
     of His thoughts and ways.

I bless you with faith expressed
     through acts of obedience
     and sacrificial love—
     with faith that is enduring and steady,
     persistent and consistent.
You will be fully alive;

you will flourish and experience joy.

Hear the word of the Lord:

Continue to live by faith.
Soon and very soon,
the One who is returning
will come without delay.

Keep God's words of promise before you:
    write them out, remember them,
    hold on to them—believe Him.
Listen to His words:

My vision, my message, is a witness
pointing to what is coming:
it hurries toward the goal,
it will not fail.
If it seems slow in coming,
wait for it: it is on its way—
it will not delay,
it will come on time.

Blessing of Believing the Unseen
Hebrews 11:1-4

In the name of Jesus Christ,
 I bless your spirit with conviction
 concerning unseen things.
May you be inspired and motivated
 from the invisible reality of Heaven.

Your faith empowers you
 to see that the universe was created
 and coordinated divinely
 by the power of God's word.
What you now see with your senses
 was not made from the visible realm.
Jesus spoke, and the invisible realm
 gave birth to the beauty you see,
 and touch, and hear, and smell, and taste.

Your faith is the only evidence required
 to prove what is still invisible.
Your faith is the substance of things you desire;
 it is the title deed, the certainty
 of things you are waiting for.

I bless you with faith operating
 so powerfully in you,
 that against all opposition and testing,
 you will remain secure in God.

Like Abel, what you believe—
 not what you bring—
 makes the difference.
Abel's belief continues to be a witness
 throughout the centuries.

I bless you with such faith,
    that your story will be heard
    down through the generations.
It's not what you have to bring—
    it's who you believe in
    and what you believe.

Blessing of Great Faith
Hebrews 11:6-7; Genesis 6:1-22

After the time of Noah, every ancient culture recorded its memory of the worldwide flood. In Noah's generation, which was ten generations after Adam and Eve, the human race had degenerated into such darkness that evil of every kind had reached epidemic proportions. The wickedness of man had become so great that "every intent" of his heart was inclined to evil (Genesis 6:4-5). The state of earth's future was at stake.

God knew one man who had a reverence and awe of Him and a pure, generational lineage: Noah. (Genesis 6:9). Most other blood-lines had become afflicted by humans interbreeding with demons. Their offspring were giants, easily motivated to perpetrate evil. They were the reason for such a degeneration of the human race. Peter Toth's book, Underestimating Satan, *helped me understand this subject.*

Faith determines whether you will experience promise. All of mankind experienced the flood, but only Noah and his family endured. He believed in God—and he and his family were saved.

In the name of Jesus Christ
    I bless your spirit with a gift of faith
    that opens up your heart
    to receive revelation from God.

Faith carries promise—
    based on a reality not yet seen.
Without faith living in you,
    you will not believe God exists,
    you won't approach Him,
    you won't seek Him.

Like Noah, step out in reverent obedience
    even when God says something
    that has never been heard before.
Press through the opposition against you—
    what looks foolish, ridiculous, naïve,
    backwards, or unprogressive to others.

Come to God in faith,
    knowing that He is real.
Your obedient act of faith
    will prove what is still unseen.

I bless you with God's deliverance—
    for your family,
    for mankind,
    for the world.

Blessing of a Walk of Faith
Hebrews 11:8-16; II Corinthians 1:18-20

Abraham's walk of faith is famous. He left his country and his family—everything. He went from the familiar to the unfamiliar. He also left with difficulty and delay because of decisions about his father and his nephew, Lot.

Garris and I have experienced five major events we called "Abraham Journeys." I have struggled and resisted going from the familiar to the unfamiliar. I have been reluctant and slow in my responses. However, my trust in God and His goodness has increased in each journey.

This blessing is written to those who never felt like they belonged—not in their family, their school, their church, or in society. You are like a foreigner living in a strange land. It's time to take a stand and come into agreement with God. It's time for a bold faith.

In the name of Jesus Christ,
    I bless your spirit with faith
    motivating you to obey God's call:
    to leave what is familiar—
    to discover the territory
    you were destined to inherit.

The evidence of your faith is God;
    He and His word are the substance—
    the certainty—of your hope.

I bless you with adventure of daring faith
    as you face the unknown with only a promise,
    not knowing your destination,
    but willing to step outside the norms
    and change the course of history.

I bless you with boldness to let go:
    no more delays,
    no more unnecessary conflict.
Step into God's faithfulness.

Like Abraham, occupy the land of promise,
    build your home there—
    foreigner or not.
Agree with God that you belong
    wherever He calls you to go
    and in whatever He calls you to do.
Even if you feel like an outsider—
    occupy the land, call it home,
    blaze a trail for others.

I bless you with a heart fixed
    on what is far greater than your
    present circumstance: God's realm.
You won't regret letting go of the past,
    you won't look back,
    you won't go back.
You can do this if you set your sights
    on the unseen City—with a real, eternal,
    unshakeable foundation—
    the City whose architect
    and builder is God Himself.

When you obey God's call,
    you inherit the promise,
    you receive Heaven's strategies,
    you take new territories.
Your obedience leads to
    new lands coming under God's rule.
God's presence and glory and authority
    will be your legacy and heritage
    to all future generations.

Blessing of the Heavenly Realm
Hebrews 11:11-19; Romans 4:13-25

Abraham would have known about human sacrifices used in pagan rituals. But with the One True God, Abraham learned something new about sacrifice. God would never require human sacrifice of death to prove allegiance and whole-hearted devotion.

Abraham had received God's promise that his wife, Sarah, would conceive a son. Through that son, Isaac, Abraham's lineage would be carried on (Genesis 21:12). Yet when it seemed like God was asking him to sacrifice his son, Abraham was willing. He had faith in God—he just didn't know what the outcome would be. He figured that God would raise Isaac from the dead. Instead, God produced a ram as a substitute sacrifice.

Symbolically, Isaac was a parable of God giving His only Son as a sacrifice for the whole world and then raising Him from the dead.

In the name of Jesus Christ,
    I bless your spirit
    with a faith so powerful
    it becomes logical
    to believe in the impossible.

As Abraham responded, I bless you
    with wholehearted devotion:
    offer God your whole heart,
    offer Him every one you love
    and everything you care about—
    give all back into the hands of God.
I bless you with belief in His goodness.

As Sarah responded,

I bless you with a faith
that embraces miraculous power
to conceive the promise.
The authority of your faith
rests in the One who made the promise—
His promise is His royal proclamation.

May you father and mother many
spiritual sons and daughters—
may they multiply
throughout the generations,
may you leave behind a mighty legacy.

Blessing of Prophetic Destiny
Hebrews 11:20-22 & 13:21

Isaac, Jacob, and Joseph are just three of many in Scripture who spoke prophetic destiny concerning the future.

God spoke and worlds were created. He has never been silent; He is always speaking. He did not begin speaking and then go silent when His written Word was finished. The Scriptures could not even contain all that transpired just in the short life span of Jesus' ministry on earth. The Bible does not contain all of God. Even the universe He created cannot contain Him.

Desire Holy Spirit gifts, especially prophecy revealed through the written and spoken words of God. Like young Samuel who said, "Speak Lord...I am listening," be listening to God's voice. He breathes His living words into your spirit. Receive His downloads of revelation, and prophesy into your generations.

In the name of Jesus Christ,
    I bless your spirit
    with God's perfecting work of grace,
    giving you all you need—
    to express through you
    all that is excellent and pleasing to Him;
    making Jesus famous.

I bless you with faith's reality
    to impart prophetic blessings
    concerning the destinies of others.
Like Isaac, who reached into the future
    as he blessed his children,
    I bless you with eyes of faith
    inspiring you to impart prophetic

vision for the future.

In an act of faith, Joseph prophesied
      Israel's future,
      and made plans for that future.
By an act of faith, may you *remember*
      what has yet to transpire
      and make plans accordingly!

Listen to the nudges of God's Spirit;
      listen to the declaration of His thoughts,
      His desires, His will expressed
      in His written and spoken words.

It is the nature of God to speak to you;
      He is vocal in His Book,
      and He is vocal everywhere else—
      He has never stopped speaking.

Jesus is the Spirit of prophecy.
I bless you with the gift of prophecy—
      with faith to impart prophetic blessings,
      impart a prophecy of promise,
      speak a prophetic word for the future—
      impacting your generation
      and all those that follow.

Blessing of Great Reward
Hebrews 11:24-31

Moses chose God's will, refusing to get his identity from being the son of the Pharaoh's daughter, despite all the privileges and wealth of that status. He chose faith in God and suffered mistreatment. He valued and believed in the promise of the coming Anointed One, who would suffer great reproach and abuse.

In the name of Jesus Christ,
    I bless your spirit with a faith so strong,
    you see beyond the present
    to make godly choices for the future.

Be motivated to act by faith.
Prefer faith's certainty
    over anything the world can offer—
    over momentary enjoyment,
    wealth or power, status or position.

Like Moses, who found his identity in God,
    and who found reward
    in God's anointing—
    even though he suffered for it,
    I bless you with your true identity.
I bless you with great reward
    that comes from God's anointing,
    even despite suffering.

There is suffering in this world
    whether you follow God or not.
If you follow Him, suffering will lead to life
    and love—instead of death.

I bless you with true hope and joy
    that involves generosity;
    a sacrificial giving.

Don't look at the present to inform you,
    but look with wonder on the ultimate:
    the Unseen God—
    faith's great reward.

I bless you with faith that stirs your heart
    to hear the word of the Lord
    and obey His directives.
I bless you with persistence—
    hold on to His word of promise.

God will act: He will fulfill His promise,
    He will prevent the destroyer
    from causing harm,
    He will deliver you into your inheritance.
Your faith will open up a way to cross over,
    your faith will release
    miraculous interventions.

I bless you with faith
    that pulls down strongholds,
    that avoids destruction,
    and provides a way of escape.

I bless you with ignited faith
    in response to God's mighty deeds.
May the power of your faith
    conquer kingdoms
    and establish true justice.
Great is your reward
    because of your faith in God.

Blessing of Endurance
Hebrews 11:32-39

The Hebrews "Hall of Fame" lists those who lived by faith in hope without receiving the fullness of their promises. Through Jesus Christ, the Messiah, God has invited us to live in faith's fullness: the fullness of promise. The faith of those who lived under the Old Covenant will come together with our faith to make one complete whole; their lives of faith complete with our faith will be brought to finished perfection.

Faith's simplest definition is to have our eyes fixed on Jesus, the author and finisher of our faith. Faith is action (looking, believing, trusting, resting in God). Faith is substance. It is a certainty about God—about His character backing His Word. When we put our trust in who He is, we can trust what He says and does.

I bless your spirit,
> in the name of Jesus Christ,
> with a faith that fastens
> onto God's promises
> and pulls them into your reality.

I bless you with faith that subdues kingdoms,
> releases righteousness,
> shuts the mouth of lions,
> puts out the power of raging fires,
> and causes many to escape certain death.

I bless you with faith to impart power
> to your weakness:
> to make you strong, to spark courage,
> to turn you into a mighty warrior in battle,
> to pull angelic armies from Heaven's realm

into battle—ready to fight with you.

Be filled with enduring faith;
    release healing to sickness
    and see the dead raised
    in resurrection power.

True faith is not an automatic exemption
    from hardship or tragedy—
    difficulties do not mean you have less faith.
The same faith that helps you escape trouble,
    sustains you to endure trouble.
The same faith that delivers some from death,
    strengthens others to die in victory.

I bless you with deep faith
    birthed in your longing expectancy
    for a glorious resurrection.
Faith will enable you to endure
    because of your trust in God;
    you will not deny your faith,
    you will be able to endure scorn,
    accusations and judgment from others,
    mockery, loss, imprisonment,
    cruel mistreatment, atrocities—even death.
The world is not worthy of you;
    it may never realize you are a true hero.

I bless you with faith's fullness:
    look away from the natural realm
    and fasten your gaze on Jesus;
    have eyes only for Him
    who sits exalted at the right hand
    of the throne of God!

I bless you with a faith that endures.

PART X:
BLESSINGS FROM JAMES, I & II PETER, I & II JOHN & REVELATION

That day in the winter of 1985 was one of the coldest since our arrival to Montana. With the wind-chill factor, it was minus 60 degrees. I had to make careful preparations before going outside in that bitter, raw, skin-damaging atmosphere.

I was running late to an appointment, and I scrambled to bundle the kids into winter gear just to get out to the car. When I finally opened the door, I turned to find my young son busy taking off his moon boots and snow suit. With frustration, I wrestled everything back on to his six-year-old body. I half-carried him through the drifts of snow to the car, strapped him in next to his sister, and started the engine to warm it.

I hurried back to the house to grab my things and lock the door. I not only felt the sting of cold reaching through my well-covered face, I also felt the familiar shame of failure as a mom. I adored my children. But being a perfect parent was not working out, no matter how hard I tried.

I was locking the door, stopping in the cold, when I heard God speak. This exchange all happened in a matter of seconds.

I heard Him very clearly say, "Thank me."

"What? What do you mean, thank you? Why would I

do that? There is nothing to be thankful for. I failed to be patient. I'm so disappointed and angry at myself."

I heard again, "Thank me."

Again, I questioned Him. I had heard clearly, but how to obey? So, I said, "Thank you, Jesus, for...?" And He responded, "Sight."

I could not grasp this. I had been intentionally practicing gratitude since high school, but obviously not to this depth. How did it help to be thankful for seeing my failure? I wanted something that would keep me from failing again. My way of changing was self-talk and increased effort for better behavior; that's how I had been making life work since I could remember. I had to admit, it was an exhausting way to force change. Not to mention that it didn't really work.

I obeyed God despite my confusion. I simply said, "Thank you, Jesus, for sight. I recognize my failure to love well." No excuses, no blaming, no self-condemning. I also did what I knew to do—I asked my son to forgive me. Our family committed to forgive each other and to ask for forgiveness.

This seemingly insignificant moment became a great catalyst for reformation. Out of a tiny step of obedience, I received an unfolding, ongoing, ever-increasing upgrade in faith.

It was one thing to have an ethereal gratitude for God—for who He was and what He had done, for what He could and would do in the future.

It was an altogether different dimension when I turned to meet with Him face to face in the middle of my mess—with gratitude! Not gratitude for my mess, but gratitude that He was right there in the mess with me.

I welcomed sight of Him surrounding me with His love. Without sight I could not identify my barriers to His love. Without sight, I remained blind to His love.

Within weeks I knew I had discovered another

treasure. Sight was the beginning of healing. Every struggle became my catalyst to turn to Jesus. I have been forever changed. Right here in the middle of my mess, I focus on His tenderness, His goodness, His mercy, and even His joy for me! My greatest goal in life is to become brilliant at receiving His love, especially at the point of my greatest need and failure.

Blessing of Wisdom
James 1:2-12

Faith is the substance and evidence of hope: it is my response to God and His word concerning something that is certain, absolute, and anchored securely in the invisible realm. I have not yet seen or experienced this certainty here on earth; the invisible has not become visible at this point, but there is no more wavering on my part. It's a done deal. I have abundance even where I perceive lack.

In the name of Jesus Christ,
    I bless your spirit with experiencing
    all the joy that you can,
    especially when it seems
    you are facing only difficulties.

God will use difficulties and troubles
    to empower you.
When your belief is tested,
    power is stirring up in you
    to endure all things.

Maturity is being released
    into every part of you,
    until nothing is missing—
    nothing is lacking.
I bless you with God's abundance.

I bless you with new perspectives—
    see an invaluable opportunity
    when your faith is tested,
    when nothing seems to go right,
    when time goes by without change,
    when there is no end in sight,

when your expectation is not met,
when trouble crouches at your door,
when there seems no way of escape.
Jesus is your pathway forward.

When you need to make a decision,
ask God for wisdom,
and He will give it to you.
He won't use your lack: your fears,
your inexperience, your failure,
as a chance to scold you or shame you.

He will overwhelm your failure
with His generous grace:
bring your doubts into the light,
be honest about indecision,
deal with disengagement,
confess half-hearted responses.
Yield your unstable heart to God,
and entrust yourself to Him.

I bless you with strong faith,
when you are encircled by difficulties:
you will continue to experience
the untold blessings of God.

True happiness comes from believing Him.
True joy comes when you receive
the victorious crown of life
promised to every lover of God!

Blessing of Continual Deliverance

James 1:19-20

In the name of Jesus Christ,
    I bless your spirit with new-found love:
    a new depth of love—
    a new life of love and freedom.
Don't postpone your joy
    in the absolute faithfulness of God!

May you grant forgiveness
    for injustice perpetrated against you
    and those you love—
    having yourself received full forgiveness.
You cannot go any further
    than your offense against others.

May you take this to heart:
    listen to God's voice,
    listen to His Word,
    listen to one another.
Be quick to listen;
    be slow to speak,
    be slow to anger.

Granting forgiveness
    does not condone wrong behavior.
Like you, God hates injustice;
    be angry at injustice,
    but don't blame God.

Don't grieve Him,
    don't go to bed angry,

don't stay angry,
don't use your anger
as fuel for revenge.
Don't give the devil
a foothold in your life.
Human anger never works
to promote God's righteous purpose.

Be forgiven, *live* forgiven—
extend forgiveness;
mercy trumps judgment.
The Word of Life has power
to continually deliver you.

Blessing of a Living Hope
I Peter 1:1-8; Psalm 36:9; Ephesians 1:3

In the name of Jesus Christ,
    I bless your spirit with getting to know—
    personally and intimately—
    the One who invited you to God.

You are not forgotten:
    you have been chosen,
    you have been destined by God,
    you have been set apart
    to be His holy one—gloriously washed
    with the blood of Jesus.

May God's delightful grace and peace
    continually flow over you,
    filling you, multiplying many times over.

Through the resurrection of Jesus Christ,
    you are reborn into a perfect inheritance:
    every spiritual blessing
    and every transcendent reality
    is promised and preserved for you
    in the heavenly realm—
    an inheritance that can never perish,
    never be defiled or diminished!

I bless you with faith worth far more than gold:
    a refined faith, an authentic faith
    that becomes a passionate love for Jesus.

Know this with great joy:
    through your faith,
    the mighty power of God

constantly guards you,
even through hardships and grief.

By believing in Him,
you are saturated with ecstatic joy—
and immersed in glory.

You have been brought into a living hope:
a hope in the power of God,
a hope of life.

Blessing of Holiness
I Peter 1:13-20; I Corinthians 1:30

*Human holiness means we are set apart for God—
absolutely devoted to God in all that we do. All the Old
Testament prophets had the Spirit of the Anointed One in
them, and they prophesied by the power of the Holy Spirit
(I Peter 1:11). Every believer in the New Covenant has the
Holy Spirit within us and everyone of us can prophesy.*

In the name of Jesus Christ,
    I bless you with shaping
    your life to become like the Holy One.
Hear His word to you:

    *You are to be holy
    because I am holy.*

I bless you with living a holy life—
    no longer forming your life
    to the desires you once had
    when you didn't know better.

May you set your life apart for God—
    may you live each day
    with holy awe and reverence,
    absolutely devoted to Him
    throughout your time on earth,
    demonstrating who He is
    to the world.
Demonstrate justice, mercy,
    truth and right living.

Grace has embedded holiness in you—
    Jesus Christ is your holiness.

May you yield to Him:
    yield to His words,
    absorb and reveal His life.

Prepare your heart and mind for action!
Share the news about your great joy:
    before the foundation of the earth was laid,
    the Messiah planned to be sacrificed
    like a spotless lamb—
    for you and the world.

It is through Jesus you now believe in God.
You are blessed with the holiness of God in you.

Blessing of God's Divine Nature
II Peter 1:3-4; Ephesians 1:3

In the name of Jesus Christ,
    I bless you with participation
    in the life of God.
His DNA—His nature—is yours;
    He shares His nature with you!

Everything you need to reflect His true nature:
    everything you need for life,
    everything you need
    for complete devotion to Him
    has been given to you, deposited in you,
    and lavished upon you.

I bless you with the wealth of knowing Him:
    He invited you to come to Him,
    He gave you His divine nature,
    He has called you by name.

I bless you with an astonishing,
    mighty, glorious manifestation
    of God's goodness.
Receive His impartation
    of magnificent promises—
    promises beyond all price.

Through the power of these tremendous
    promises, you can partner
    with God's divine nature:
    He is your Father.
He empowers you to escape corruption
    by His divine nature.
You are acquitted, reborn, brought forth,

and now growing up as His child,
through the astounding revealing
of His presence and goodness.

You are blessed with every spiritual blessing
    contained in Heaven.
Everything Heaven contains
    is already poured out on you—
    love gifts from your wonderful Father.

It is His nature to be good;
    It is your nature to receive His goodness.

Blessing of Activation
II Peter 1:5-9; Matthew 5:8; Colossians 1:27

Although you already have qualities of God's nature in abundance, you must activate them.

I bless your spirit,
    in the name of Jesus Christ,
    with devotion to activate
    the qualities of His nature
    already in your possession,
    already planted deeply in you,
    already growing up from within—
    continuously abundant
    and more than enough.

I bless you with lavish additions
    to your basic faith:
    with supplements that fit together
    and complement each other.

Activate what you have been given
    by adding goodness of character—
    the integrity of walking in the light,
    the diligence to act with moral valor,
    the courage to give honor and live honorably.

The purifying of your character
    brings blessings—
    you are blessed with seeing God;
    with understanding His heart for you—
    His goodness, His ways of thinking,
    His power to effect change.

Good character plus understanding of God

develops your inner strength—
a strength directly from God's strength:
a power to persevere, to have self-control,
to be disciplined.

Understanding plus inner strength
trains you for passionate,
patient endurance.
Endurance trains you for godliness;
a reverent wonder and devotion to God.

Godliness increases your heart of mercy
for your brothers and sisters.
Mercy develops and trains you
for generous love.
I bless you with multiple graces
to flourish in each of these dimensions.

If you are not experiencing growth
in these qualities,
you still live under condemnation—
searching to be forgiven
of your original sins.

Remember you have been made innocent—
Jesus Christ lives in you,
and you share in His glory.
You are blessed with the full riches
of His presence.

Blessing of a Firm Footing
II Peter 1:8-11; Zephaniah 3:17; Philippians 4:8

In the name of Jesus Christ,
    I bless your spirit
    in your pursuit of knowing Him
    more intimately.

Remember—you have been made innocent;
    your past sins have been washed away.
This is the mystery of your faith:
    Christ in you, your hope of glory.

I bless you with a joy and eagerness
    to confirm and validate
    God's invitation of salvation.

He spoke and you were His;
    He claims you as His own.
You are a *chosen word* from His mouth;
    you will not return void,
    you will accomplish
    what He has destined for you.

May you devote yourself to God
    by activating His character in you,
    and standing firm with Him.

As a result, you will never stumble—
    the true Lord of the Dance
    is full of joy for you:
    He calms you with His love,
    He delights you with His songs,
    He has choreographed your steps—
    your life will be on a firm footing;

you will walk on paved streets
and wide pathways.

Jesus the Messiah welcomes you
into His eternal Kingdom:
He brought His Kingdom to earth
and opened wide the Kingdom gates to you.

Blessing of Biblical Prophecy
II Peter 1:16-21; Matthew 17:1-13; Malachi 4:2 & 5

Scriptural prophecy is not some fantasy or human imagination. The prophecies we read in Scripture can be interpreted through other Scriptures.

On the Mount of Transfiguration, God once again confirmed Scriptural prophecies about His Son, Jesus the Messiah, who would bring His eternal Kingdom to earth. The words of the Old Testament prophets were made more certain by this astounding experience.

The appearance of Moses and Elijah confirmed that the Law and the Prophets support Jesus and His mission of redemption. Jesus' disciples witnessed and experienced and recorded this confirmation.

In the name of Jesus Christ,
    I bless your spirit
    with His testimony
    of the Father's endorsement.

The Father unveiled His Son's
    splendor and magnificence,
    lavishing radiant glory
    and honor upon Him, saying:

This is my cherished Son,
in whom I am fulfilled.
He is marked by my love—
all my delight is found in Him,
and my favor rests on Him!

When you hear of the power
    and appearing of Jesus Christ,
    you are not being told

some masterfully crafted legend,
some fairy tale or fantasy.
These prophecies do not originate
from human initiative
or someone's imagination—
these prophecies are truth.

God's message is the promise
of His piercing power and light
shinning into the darkness,
bathing it in the light of truth—
displacing the dismal gloom.

God's cherished Son, Jesus,
the Sun of Righteousness,
has risen with healing in His wings,
with radiant beams of light
streaming outward in all directions—
each beam of brilliant light
flowing with healing;
restoration of health,
deliverance and rescue,
peace and refreshing.

May you experience God's promise
of redemption and love:
His promise of eternal salvation,
His promise of a new day rising
within your heart
like the dawning of the morning star,
like the dawn conquering the night.

Blessing of the Life-Giver
I John 1:1-4; Acts 17:26-28

In the name of Jesus Christ,
    I bless your spirit with vision of the One
    who has existed from before the beginning—
    the Living Expression of God.
Jesus lives face to face with the Father
    and now He is face to face with you.

I bless you with sight of Jesus:
    hear the melody of His heart,
    listen to His life giving words,
    experience His presence—
    feel what motivates Him.

Your Life-Giver has made a way for you.
You don't have to grope around in the dark—
    search for Him and you will find Him;
    He's right there beside you.

May your spirit know the reality of Jesus.
In Him you live and move
    and have your being—
    you are God-created!

I bless you with true fellowship
    and partnership with the Father
    and with His Son,
    Jesus the Anointed One.
I release to you fullness of joy.

Blessing of Pure Light
I John 1:5-7

Freedom from sin is living with nothing hidden; it is living in the light.

In the name of Jesus Christ,
    I bless your spirit with light
    illuminating your darkness.
God is pure light—you will never find
    a trace of darkness in Him:
    His message is life-giving,
    His words are true.

I bless you with unbroken fellowship:
    living with nothing hidden,
    living in the pure light
    that surrounds Jesus.

Then you will have everything
    in common with Him—
    sharing what He has,
    sharing who He is—
    you will be close,
    intimate, true friends.

I bless you with an open, transparent,
    and honest relationship with God.
You are completely forgiven,
    but you will reap the effects
    of what you sow.
Rebellion against Him and His law of love
    affects your intimacy and friendship
    with Him and with others.

There is a solution for sin—call it sin.
Jesus will wash you clean
 of the cause and effects of your actions;
 you will experience restoration
 of what you lost,
 you will experience renewal.

I bless you with ongoing freedom from sin.
Walk continuously in the light—
 live in the pure light of Jesus.

Blessing of Intimacy
I John 2:3-6

In the name of Jesus Christ,
    I bless your spirit
    with truly knowing God—
    with experiencing
    greater depths of love and intimacy.

May you keep God's words
    because you love Him,
    because you love what He says.

Just obeying God's words,
    by regulation and rules
    doesn't mean that you know Him.
But obeying God's words
    is the evidence of knowing Him.
You cannot know Him
    if you don't obey Him.

I bless you with experiencing
    the mature love of God
    being perfected in you.

Don't just say *I am intimate with God;*
    truly *live* in intimacy with God,
    because you walk
    in the footsteps of Jesus.

Blessing of God's Blazing Light
I John 2:7-11

In the name of Jesus Christ,
    I bless your spirit with true light—
    the light of God's love
    shining through Jesus—
    the light that is destroying darkness.

When God's light exposes darkness in you,
    He is faithful to forgive every time;
    His forgiveness is just,
    and He will continue to cleanse you
    because of His Son, Jesus.

When you live in the light,
    you won't be haunted by fear,
    you won't step into a trap,
    you won't be blinded by darkness,
    you won't live in darkness—
    stumbling around or causing
    anyone else to stumble.
When you live in the light,
    you will glow with His glory.

I bless you with love for the light—
    darkness will disappear,
    and you will live
    in the blazing light of God.

Blessing of Courageous Faith
I John 2:12-17; Revelations 12:10-11

In the name of Jesus Christ,
    I bless your spirit
    with remembrance.
Remember: your sins
    have been forever removed
    because of the power of Jesus' name.
Remember: you have a true relationship
    with the Father—
    the One who has existed
    from before the beginning.
Remember: you are strong;
    you have defeated the evil one
    because of your union with Jesus,
    and you have treasured
    His word in your heart.

The love of the world and the love
    of the Father are incompatible;
    don't set the affections
    of your heart on this world,
    set them on Him.

The world offers gratification,
    the allurement of things,
    and the obsession with status.
But these systems and structures
    and this world order,
    that leave God out of the picture,
    are disappearing.

I bless you with a love to continually
    and habitually do the will of God.

Blessing of Anointing
I John 2:20-28

In the name of Jesus Christ,
    I bless your spirit with truth.
You have the capacity to know the truth;
      He has anointed you to know truth,
      and no lie belongs to the truth.

To embrace the truth, embrace Jesus Christ,
      and you will be embracing the Father.
I bless you with close friendship
      with Jesus and with the Father;
      in Him, you will live your life in truth,
      you will live in promise,
      you will have never-ending life.

If you fear deception or being led astray,
      remember: you have received
      God's anointing.
His anointing is so much greater
      than any deception;
      His anointing teaches you
      all that you need to know
      and leads you into all truth.
His anointing lives in you.

May you remain in His anointing
      so that when He is revealed—
      both now and upon His return—
      you will respond with confident joy.

Blessings of Pursuit
Revelation 3:20; Psalm 23:6; Ezekiel 37:1-14

In the name of Jesus Christ,
    I bless your spirit with belief
    in His faithful mercies,
    His multiple kindnesses,
    and His eternal love for you.

Jesus is knocking on your heart's door—
    hear Him deep in your innermost being,
    in those closed-off chambers.
He is waiting expectantly
    for you to let Him in.
May you dare to open that part
    of your heart to Him.

I speak to lost childhood, lost innocence,
    lost time, lost joy, lost trust—
    come, Breath of God:
    breathe on those desolate places of the heart—
    blow the fresh wind of your Spirit,
    breath your newness of life.

Come, Breath of Life:
    breathe on this crushed heart:
    empty, wounded by exposure,
    shamed and ridiculed.
Breathe on the fractures
    cracked by loneliness,
    breathe on the remnant shards of battle
    laying shredded, scattered,
    and abandoned.

Come, Breath of God:

breathe your resurrection life—
your glory, your visible Presence,
breathe certainty of your favor,
breathe your promise and provision,
breathe hope of future goodness.

I speak to any false belief
that you are not worth
being passionately pursued
and extravagantly loved.
May God's word pierce your heart
and impart truth;
He pursues you with His goodness
and mercy all the days of your life.

I bless you with a greater longing for God
than your need to secure your own safety—
greater than your determination
to never trust again.
I bless you with pursuit of Him
in response to His relentless pursuit of you.

EPILOGUE

In my twenties, I started recognizing more clearly my fear of failure. I was afraid to look at my failure even though it stared me in the face. When I was forced to see, I had no real solution except to try harder to succeed. I had spent a lifetime relying on myself to be strong, smart, capable, and responsible. But the harder I worked at meeting the standard I had set, I was never enough; I was either raising the bar or failing to meet the bar.

In 1979, a dear friend and neighbor, Linda Abblett, asked me if I would attend a women's Bible study with her, not far from my home. I agreed to go. Not long after joining the study group, I got a call from the leader, Kathy Gilbert, asking me if I would consider leading the worship time each week. I think I responded calmly enough and answered with a standard, "I would like to pray about it before answering"—but on the inside I went into a panic. "No, no, no!" was my reaction.

Garris and I had recently started attending Faith Center Church in Eugene, Oregon. We had both experienced an encounter with God and were profoundly and forever impacted. Our hearts opened to entrust ourselves to His Lordship, and we said "yes" to truly following Him. Garris entered Faith Center's school of ministry and I attended part-time, while raising our children.

What if God was asking me to say "yes" to leading worship for our study group? Kathy was extremely talented and gifted in her singing. She was also anointed in her calling and passion as a worship leader. Who was I? I had not been attending the study for very long. I had never led a worship time. I didn't know any of their songs. And I couldn't sing well! I was new to the church, new to living empowered by the Holy Spirit, and new to worship in the Spirit.

I was terrified—so I fasted and prayed and wrestled and wrangled with my insecurity and sheer fear. On the fourth day of fasting, I was in a worship service at Faith Center when I finally could hear God. He said, "Would you be willing?" He was giving me a choice. He wasn't demanding anything. I desired to follow God more than to give into the fear of making a fool of myself, so I said "yes."

I had one week to learn some songs. I sang while cleaning the dishes, while playing with my two babies—basically all throughout the day. I was struck with how close I felt to God. There was something about focusing attention on Him and declaring His heart and His truth. He was filling up my dry spirit and soul.

On the day before the Bible study, I lost my voice completely. I was young and unschooled in the subject of fear and its physical impact, but the sudden loss of my voice illustrates the degree of my fear. I called Kathy and whispered my dilemma. She had no idea what I was going through, but her response was wise. If I was unable to sing or speak by the study time, I could try to start the song and she would carry it for me. If I could not make a sound, she would cover for me.

I arrived the following day speaking in only a whisper. But when I opened my mouth to begin a song, I could sing—every song. My choices of songs, without knowing the Scripture being taught that morning, fit the direction Holy Spirit was taking us.

At the end of the study, without a voice I whispered my goodbyes, still gripped in fear. There was a new element, however—an awe of God. So right there in the car, on my drive home, I began whispering thanks to God for helping me that day. I thanked Him for the grace He gave me to risk stepping out. I thanked Him for identifying my fear and pride. I thanked Him for giving me a voice to sing, and even more—for helping me to hear His voice in choosing songs that fit His purpose.

I made a choice that day to be willing to face the many fears that immobilized me. From that day, I started thanking God for delivering me from fear and training me for freedom, before I even entered possible conflict. If I knew there might be opposition or judgment, I forgave ahead of time. After all, He had forgiven me before I could ever respond to Him.

I will be forever grateful for that Bible study. I didn't know it, but with just one step of obedience, I gave God permission to train and prepare me in a safe and loving environment for a future assignment. Not long later, Garris and I would be pioneering a church in Kalispell, Montana, and I would be part of the worship team (beginning with just the two of us). I led worship—or helped lead— for many small groups and retreats over the years.

There is nothing quite so hopeful and joyful and peaceful as being free from fear—free to receive and give love. I continue to ask Jesus to tear down obstacles and barriers to His love.

PRAYER RESOURCE

In 1979, I started to become more intentional about expressing gratitude in the middle of difficulty. The following simple prayers were born in struggles over many years. The prayers started out as what are now the italicized opening lines to each section below.

It took me fifteen years to learn these, mostly while raising my children. I discovered that what I wanted them to know about God, I wasn't experiencing for myself. I would say to my three-year-old, "God doesn't love you less when you do something wrong. And God doesn't love you more, when you do everything perfectly. Daddy and I feel the same way." Then I would hear Abba whisper to me, "I feel the same way about you."

I am naturally a problem solver. That tendency to solve and fix things carried over into trying to fix myself. But ultimately, I've never been able to fix myself, much less fix someone else.

My neighbor, Linda, and I prayed regularly together early mornings before our children awoke. One morning we met to pray in the basement of my house. During a time of listening, I had a vision. I saw a brilliant light consuming darkness all around me.

I also became aware that the Light was highlighting something, and my eyes were drawn to it. On the ground next to me was something dark and definitely not good. I reacted by scooping it up and tossing it out. But, in doing so, I created a hole just as dark: so I kept digging. The more I dug, the harder it got, and the hole got deeper and darker and uglier. Although it was imperative to remove what felt and looked really yucky, I realized that I had dug myself into the hole.

I then heard, "Stop—look at the Light." I looked up out of the hole and was again conscious of light, and only the light. I heard in my spirit. "I spotlighted that darkness so that you could see it, but only long enough to immediately turn to me and bring it to me. I'll take it from you. No more digging. Keep your focus on Me."

And so I did. I found myself out of the hole, my eyes only on the light. My hands were open, holding the ugly, dark stuff. What I held out to Him was suddenly no longer there. It was exposed in the light and became light.

No more digging on my own; no more self-rescue. What Jesus highlighted for me to see was just enough. Years later, I learned how to intentionally process any issue He highlighted by learning to listen to Him and to follow His lead.

My goal is to use sight of any struggle to immediately—or as quickly as possible—fix my sights on Jesus, who is right there with me. He is not squeamish about being close to me and my stuff—in fact, He is glad we are so close! The key for me is being grateful for His mercy—His refusal to leave me stuck in my mess.

God is not impatient or angry with me. He's not "out there" somewhere, distant and uninvolved. He is right here loving me, training me to overcome. I am no longer a victim. I no longer want to grieve Him by pushing Him away—often unconsciously—until I can get my act together.

Prayers for Hope & Joy

1.
Jesus, thank you for sight —
I'm trying to make life work without you.
I'm relying on myself—
working hard to prove my worth.
I see why I feel so distant from you—
I've not received your love
in this part of my heart!
Where there is fear, love is lacking;
thank you for opening my eyes to your love.

2.
Sight is the beginning of healing —
sight is your invitation to come to you,
into the light.
Your power to transform
is found only in the light.
To be near you is to live in the light.

3.
Keep giving me sight —
there is no end to your love,
but fear always stands in the way.
I will celebrate you—
you are right here with me,
right beside me in this mess,
your arm around me.
I invite your brilliant beauty
into every hurting, fearful,
angry part of my heart.

4.
What you did was enough!
You carried my guilt and shame and me

to the grave and raised me up—reborn.
You are the Flowing Fountain of life—
your blood flows continuously over me,
cleansing me, covering me, enveloping me.

5.
I cannot add one thing to your sacrifice—
no act of penance,
no strain of self-saving effort,
no self-condemnation to make myself right.
You paid the price for my rebellion;
you took my punishment and shame—
you were the only one who could pay—and live.

I was blind, but now I can see you:
I see my desperate need for you,
I see you removed all obstacles
standing between us,
I see the raw, crushing beauty of Calvary,
I see a glimpse of your incomprehensible love.

6.
Jesus, I cannot change myself,
but your unfailing kindnesses
draw me to you—transforming me.

7.
Jesus, your love for me is unchanging—
you don't love me more
when I succeed,
when I am strong,
or when I am right.
You don't love me less when I fail,
when I am weak,
when I am sick,
when I am under attack.

Your love overflows in abundance—full on.

8.
It is your mercy that I have sight—
I can see what is broken, ruined, lost—
not to receive blame
but to remove my barriers of shame,
to open my blinded eyes to your love.
Your power is expressed in the light.

9.
Jesus, you are good—
You are good to me.
I renounce any lie I believe that
because of my troubles,
because of this chaotic world,
because life does not feel good,
because things are not good—
that *you* must not be good.
I renounce my judgment against you:
you are good to me all the time,
and I can trust you.

Jesus, I am the one you love.
Forgive me for not believing
in your love for me.
I renounce all self-hated and self-judgment;
I renounce critical judgments toward others.

I speak to all ungodly beliefs—
all self-protective thinking,
my right to myself,
my independence and rebellion,
my ways of making life work without you.
I speak to all destructive cellular memories,
all physical manifestation of illness or disease,

and I say: come into the light of Jesus Christ,
come into alignment with His truth.
I command deliverance and healing.

Abba, I receive your fathering presence,
your protection and provision.
Holy Spirit, I receive your nurture and comfort,
your kindness and tenderness,
your instructions for life—your love.
Jesus, I receive your friendship
and companionship,
your strength to overcome and rise up,
your authority and power.
I receive.
I am eternally thankful!

Made in the USA
San Bernardino, CA
09 March 2018